GOD HAS A
PURPOSE
WITH YOU

A journey through dreams and
reality that will help you find
God´s purpose for your life.

ROBERT GREEN

FOREWORD BY CHRISTINE D´CLARIO

God bless you. I hope this book is a blessing for your life. Remember that despite the ups and downs, God has a purpose with you. Att: Robert Green

For: _____

GOD HAS A PURPOSE WITH YOU

ROBERT GREEN

Edition: August 2021
Copyright ©2020 by Robert Green.
ISBN: 978-1-9566-2538-7
All rights reserved. This publication may not be reproduced, partially or totally altered, filed, copied, downloaded or distributed, by any printed or digital means, without the prior written permission of the author.

Unless otherwise indicated, all Scriptures quotations are taken from the New King James Version, ©1979,1980, 1982, 1984 by Thomas Nelson, Inc. Used by permission. All rights reserved. Scripture quotations marked (KJV) are taken from the King James Version of the Holy Bible. Used with permission. Scriptures marked (NIV) are taken from The Holy Bible, New International Version®, NIV®, Copyright © 1999 by Biblica, Inc.® Used with permission. Scriptures marked "NLT" are taken from the Holy Bible, New Living Translation, © Tyndale House Foundation, 2010. Used with permission. Scripture quotations marked (NASB) are taken from the Holy Bible, New American Standrad Bible, 1995, 2020. LaHabra, CA: The Lockman Foundation. Scripture Quotes (TLA) are taken from Current Language Translation ™ © United Bible Societies, 2002, 2004. Bold text in Bible quotes represents the author's emphasis.

Author: Robert Green – Independent Author.
Editing and Proofreading: Carlos Arturo Guisarre, Vianny Solano, Sinai Urdaneta and Gisela Sawin.
Cover Design: David Navejas | DNG Creative.
Design Covers and Memoirs: Sinai Urdaneta | Seven Media
General Layout: Euselandia Alcántara | ERASDG.
Editorial Agency: ERAS Disgraf, Llc., Miami, Florida | MDConexiones.

This book is available in electronic format - Amazon Kindle.
Printed in the United States of America.
Author Contact: contacto@robertgreenb.com
www.robertgreenb.com

ROBERT GREEN

«In the last days we will see a great spiritual awakening like never before, where millions of believers will experience the glory of God to a level that hasn't been seen on the Earth yet. As you read this, I hope you experience in your heart a burning desire to become not only a spectator of what God will do with others, but a protagonist and a partner in God's story. My friend Robert Green has the grace and passion needed to inspire us to know more about the eternal purpose, so that we may all be conformed to the image of the Son, and we may please the Father in everything (Romans 8:29).»

Marcos Brunet • TOMATULUGAR Ministry

«We can make many great discoveries in life, such as: who am I going to marry, what career should I study, where am I going to live, etc. These are just a few of the pieces that make up our life purpose. But my friend Robert Green discovered the most important thing: God's purpose for his life. For this reason, his story can be a mirror in which we can all see our reflections. I am convinced that my friend has been able to endure the processes he has had to go through because he was covered by a strength that comes only from God. I also know that he has persevered because that same God revealed His purpose to him, and when you already know what is ahead of you, the waiting gets easier. Finding out our purpose is powerful and effective because it reveals the reason for our existence. I have always admired Robert Green's incredible talent, and I recognize God's anointing in his life. I invite you to read this book, knowing in advance that *God has a purpose with you* that will bless you.»

Willy Gonzáles • REDIMI2

«I met my friend Robert at a worship activity. While he was ministering to the Lord and singing along with the Barak team, God's glory cloud descended and when Robert guided us to set out eyes only on Jesus and not be distracted from Him, we all immediately turned our affection to God, and the embrace of His Presence was so tangible that it was shocking. I could see the authority that there is over his life, and I understood that "every glory has a story". I thank God for this book; his honesty and vulnerability are reflected in every word, every chapter, every testimony told. I am convinced that it will be a great blessing to anyone who reads it. Thank you, Robert, for not giving up and for telling the whole world that GOD HAS A PURPOSE for each of us!»

Josh Morales • Miel San Marcos

«Robert Green is one of the biggest and most special gifts that God has given this generation. If you allow him, the message that he carries and the life that he irradiates will mark your life forever. These are not pages filled with mere information, this is a manual that guides a whole generation back to God and helps them find their purpose! What a timely message! We have never needed this word more than we do today. Without any doubt, this book will set a precedent in your life. Buckle up and join the thousands that are already part of this message and movement!»

Bryce Manderfield • *Founder and President of Soluciones Juveniles, Inc.*

«My dear Robert´s life has been a huge blessing since the moment I met him. God, in His mercy, has freed us from all condemnation of our past through His wonderful love, care and the way that He has called us. I know that this book will violently challenge us to find our purpose while going through Robert's advice and testimonies. I pray that the Holy Spirit takes every single written word from this book and transforms it into life for each one of us.»

Alex Campos

«I've always admired the four Gospels from the Bible, because they tell the same story but in different ways. Each of them tells us about the life and ministry of our Lord Jesus Christ, and how His great power transformed the lives of so many. Reading my friend's book is "as if" he was writing his own fifth Gospel from his own life experiences and narrating how Jesus' power transformed him and gave him purpose. There are three voices that will try to give direction to your life: your own voice, the enemy's voice, and other people's voices; but the voice that overcomes and prevails over every other voice is the one of our heavenly Father - the Creator of the Universe and the author of the purpose for your life. Without any doubt, this book will take you back to the arms of the Father and will bless you.»

Daniel Calveti

«I've read stories of many great men from the different areas of society and it's interesting to know them through their own experiences and biographies, but it's a different thing when you know someone's story and then you read it in a book, because it's the recounting of the different situations someone you love has experienced, so you can see everything from another perspective. It is amazing to see a friend fighting to become better every day and to understand that these stories will be read by many, as I was able to walk with him through many of the things that he describes. That is priceless. At his young age, Robert is a fighter. He had a dream since he was a boy and nothing was able to stop him; neither poverty, nor hunger, nor the different situations he had to face could beat him. There was a "Dreamer warrior" flame in his heart that knew where he was going and what he was fighting for. This book is a journey that will take you to a new level and will help you see life from a different perspective. Only then you will understand there is nothing impossible if you are able to believe in God and in yourself.»

Angelo Frilop • Barak band

«I'm sure this book will be a tool to raise young people all over the world with a heart willing to lay down every personal plan to give God control of their lives. In this book you will find broken pieces that fell in the hands of God to create a masterpiece. I know that Robert Green's process will reveal to us how God draws us near with His love strings even if we walk away from Him, because He has a purpose with you. Without doubt, you will find the tools you need to examine yourself and find the plan that God designed for you; not for your own goals, but for the ones that come from Him. After reading this book, you will experience a burning desire to seek the Presence of God in intimacy. I hope you enjoy this beautiful testimony of life as much as I did.»

Janiel Ponciano • Barak band

«I met Robert Green during that part of our story when not many people would dare to give a prophetic word about our destiny or purpose in life, because even if God has plans for us, it's a big challenge to see and believe in them. The thing is diamonds cannot be found if you have only seen them polished and displayed in a showcase; you need to seek on deep lands to find them. That is the difference. It is possible that many ignore the fact that something ordinary and opaque could then have so much value.

But only mentors, the specialists, can tell the difference between valueless stones and diamonds in the rough, and we walk them through the transformation process into becoming valuable components before God's eyes.

This reminds me of so many people in the Bible who seemed like they did not have a chance to succeed in life, but then became the owners of entire kingdoms. Like David: spurned by everyone, inadequate under the eyes of his brothers and father, yet he was a crucial piece to God's purpose.

I want to invite everyone who has a dream, those who believe in God's purpose for their lives, to read this book because it will be of great help during that season where very few people believe in what you know you are and ignore what God can do. *God has a purpose with you* will help you keep God's dream alive inside of you and will give you principles to make it happen. Remember that many people have just one goal in life, and that is to kill the plan that God prepared for you. This book will be the map that will help you arrive to your destination and secure GOD'S PURPOSE FOR YOUR LIFE.»

Pres. Santiago and Morelys Ponciano
• *Spiritual parents*

«It's such an honor for me that my son Robert can testify to others what God has done in his life and how the Lord has guided his path. A couple of days before writing this, someone told me that he had heard Robert say he "didn't know how not to be a Christian". I do not know it either, but I have always known that being one is the greatest treasure of all. For this reason, Proverbs 22:6 were the words that went through my mind and heart daily for my three children. I'm sure that when reading these pages, you'll be able to see God and His Word fighting for a son of the promise.»

Dr. Ramon Green. My father

«The book you hold in your hands, written by my eldest son, Robert Green, is about overcoming the different spiritual and behavioral problems to emerge victorious from fear and anxiety by seeing a real God in every circumstance of your life. *God has a purpose with you* was born in the heart of a young man whose purpose is to teach you that, although obstacles always arise, God wants to bless you. Its author encourages you to remain in the faith, and victory will come to you and take you to another level (Romans 8:37). I invite you to read this wonderful book with great attention, for it will guide you to understand why trials come, and how to go through them to achieve your purpose.»

Dr. Maria Brito. My mother

«I know that every sentence of this book will bless your life, just as it has blessed mine. I am so very proud of you, my dear Robert, and of how God has shaped you all this time. I could see your life reflected in each chapter, and I watched how God marked a "before and after" in you. You are an example of perseverance, courage, and how processes can make you stronger and stronger. Through each page I could really feel your heart. I have always thought I knew you, but when I read God has a purpose with you, I could feel you in a deeper way, I could perceive your pain and your longings, and how God has worked in your life. I recognized that He has stood behind you in your battles by understanding how you truly love Him. This is just the beginning of everything that God wants to show you and everything that He will do in your life. I am more than blessed to have you by my side and to be able to call you, my husband. You're an example to me and your children.»

Ana Polanco • My wife

Content

	Acknowledgments	13
	Foreword	17
	Introduction	21
CHAPTER 1	An upside-down house	25
CHAPTER 2	The father's image	37
CHAPTER 3	The gifts God has given me	51
CHAPTER 4	Intimacy with The Holy Spirit	63
CHAPTER 5	God has bigger dreams!	79
	Memories	97
CHAPTER 6	Wise decisions	113
CHAPTER 7	Deposits in the heart of God	131
CHAPTER 8	The challenge of a crisis	145
CHAPTER 9	Sleep, sing and travel	163
CHAPTER 10	There's a sound in you	181
	Before we finish…	195

Acknowledgments

To You, my God, for giving me Your great love and mercy, for being my daily inspiration, for choosing me despite my many flaws, and for giving purpose, direction, and destiny to my life when not many people believed in me. For sustaining my faith and extending Your hand when in multiple occasions I wanted to run in the opposite direction. For being the main character of these ten chapters, and for inspiring and teaching me every time that I sat down to write - You were not only my companion, but you were also my guide. Without You I want nothing, for I know that with You I have everything I need. Your grace is enough.

Anny, you have been my support in difficult times and a handkerchief for my tears in every one of my processes, the voice of God when I needed to listen to Him, my eternal girlfriend, my wife, and the one who takes my victories as if they were her own. Thank you, my love, for always being in the front row taking pictures and enjoying my concerts, as well as being the first one to correct me and motivate me when I am not doing it right! With you, all my sorrows fade away and I soar to a world of happiness when I am by your side. I love you and I will love you forever. My queen. My perfect complement.

Amy, Jayden, and Dylan, you are the fulfillment of God's promises for my life - my greatest gift and blessing. You can make me mad and put a smile on my face from one second to the next one. Your daddy loves you and I hope that the tools in this book help you discover your purpose in life, and you can carry on with dignity the legacy of faith that I am leaving you. I cannot promise that dad will be around for the rest of your lives, but I do promise to help you and love you for the rest of mine. I love you and I am proud of you!

Mommy, you are my superhero. I could write a whole book just telling how much I love you and how grateful I am for everything that you have done for me. You are my greatest inspiration, and so you are to everyone who gets to know you. For ever and ever, my overcomer.

Dad, I would not have been able to write this book without your wise advice and the seeds that you have sowed in my heart. Thanks for instructing me, loving me, praying, and asking God that the same Robertico that one day walked hand in hand with you declaring your poetry, would now be a great man of God. I love you, daddy! Although it was not easy, you did it.

Little sisters, Catherine, and Caroline, I love you. Do you remember all the crazy things we did together? Like when we used to play marbles and basketball, or when we sang and slid on the balcony. I will never forget when we played soccer with our pillows and used the sheets to slide on the stairs. We laughed and told stories until we fell asleep. I give thanks every day for having the best sisters in the world, who have made me so happy since my childhood.

Ibel, my dear mother-in-law, I thank God so much for your life; you have known how to believe in me and support me from day one. Thanks to my father-in-law, Gilberto, and my sisters-in-law, Marlenne and Gibe. I ended up being quite a good catch, right?

Cheers to those afternoons having fun on the beaches of Nagua and Bethel 6 #26.

Angelo and Raquel, thank you for being such a blessing to me and for being present in one of the most crucial moments of my life by bringing me hope and a lot of strength in a season where I did not have any. I love you, friends!

Janiel, God remembered to give me the brother I asked for a long time ago. Josué, David, Ismael Davila and Pao, you have been there since the beginning; this story would not be written without you. Thank you for always being close to me!

Pastors Santiago and Norelis Ponciano, you have been, and you are the voice of many prophetic words that I have received in the last twenty-five years. I am inspired and moved by your personal commitment and faithfulness to God. Thank you for watching over and sustaining my spiritual life!

My beloved church, TBA. What a great family God has given me! I am more than proud of your passion and work so that the world can experience and encounter God.

Sinaí, we can finally celebrate, my friend! Only you and I will know about the countless hours we spent editing and correcting. Even when I would have just given up, you helped me find the words I needed to communicate my story. Thank you, my friend!

Thanks to everyone who has been with me, no matter the time and space this journey took. To those friends who were there when this was just a dream, and to those who have become part of my present by sharing or commenting on a video, a piece of writing or a photo. To those who have attended a concert, who have hugged me in an airport, in the streets, in a hotel lobby, or anywhere else. To those who have sent me an e-mail full of blessings, who have encouraged me to keep going, who have prayed for me, those who have defended me, who have questioned me, who have taught me and corrected me.

To you, reader, and friend, who honors me by being here, eager to read this book. God bless you!

Foreword

You probably chose this book because you admire the gifts God has placed in Robert Green's life. Without a doubt, the Lord has gifted our generation by giving us Robert's inspiring songs and amazing voice. I met Robert through his musical ministry, as a singer of the Barak band. Over the years I have been greatly blessed by the anointing of God that rests upon him. But by getting to know him, I have noticed that his life reaffirms that popular proverb that says: "There's always a story behind the glory". Many times, that story is forged in fire. And Robert Green knows about this.

Christianity has been a part of my life for as long as I can remember. I was born and raised in a home with a fervent belief in a living God - one that has become real many times in our household. This is a huge blessing and privilege, but also a great challenge. It is something that the author of this wonderful book, Robert Green, and I have in common.

One would think that if you live in a Christian home everything is easier. I have even heard many people say that a great "testimony" is to have lived a life without God and, after a supernatural encounter with Him, experiencing a drastic change that transforms a life. By the way, there is no doubt that these stories are powerful.

But it is just as powerful to hear testify someone who, even after being brought up in a Christian home, in the very house of Salvation, was close to getting lost if Christ would not have encountered him.

He He who was able to decipher the sound of the divine voice of the Holy Spirit amidst the loud religious chatter that may exist among His followers is the one who truly understands that being raised surrounded by church benches does not guarantee you an automatic trip to salvation. You need to find redemption in the God of the Gospel and have a personal relationship with Him. We all have an intrinsic and unquenchable need that only God can meet.

God has a purpose with you iis a book that reveals the way God has been forming His purpose in Robert Green's life, even using the difficult moments to shape his true identity as a son of God. In his account, he narrates the process of discovering that his identity was not found in his upbringing, but in his Creator. It should be clarified that growing up under the guardianship of a father who is also a pastor, passionate about the guarding of his sheep, and a mother fiercely in love with God, resulted in him having a heart devoted to the service of God. However, it also raised some big questions: How to face the pressures that come from being "a pastor's kid"? How to overcome the difficult trials faced by those who are raised in a family of church leaders? Moreover, what to do when fulfilling ecclesiastical dogmas puts the unity of a family in danger? And finally, how do I find God's purpose in my challenges?

I was surprised to read Robert Green's answer to these and other essential questions in life. This wonderful book encloses the wisdom that Robert Green has acquired through the way he was brought up by his family, and the path to discovering, developing, and using his gifts to lift high the name of Jesus in the nations with the help of his ministry.

In addition to a personal story, the author's honesty will be - without doubt - a guide to anyone who wants to find his purpose in God, along with his personal story or specific calling.

After being born, we all go through a continuous cycle of suffering, healing, learning, and growing. This book shows and illustrates how God uses this process time and time again to refine His character and purpose in our life. You will find numerous keys for your own growth in each of these pages.

I pray that, once you finish reading this book, you may receive as much blessing and inspiration as I have received. And that the "story behind the glory" that is being forged in your life may produce more and more of the shining light of Christ in you. My wish for you is that you will be blessed knowing that God has a purpose with you.

Christine D' Clario

Introduction

God created everything that exists with the sound of His voice. With a few words, He gave origin, substance, and purpose to everything that our eyes can see. It took Him a couple of days to create what we now know as galaxies, sky, earth, animals, and everything else we appreciate. However, He realized He could not rest until He had finished His masterpiece: creating the human being. And that's where you and I come into the picture. We are that special piece that completes God's plan with the mission of reflecting the Father over everything that has already been created; that's because He created us to look so much like Him.

Unfortunately, we are not always able to see our reflection in God's clean mirror to see the reasons why we live and exist. I know - there might have been thousands of circumstances that made you feel disengaged and different from God's perfection, which seems so out of reach, but this fact does not actually erase you from His mind and let alone, from His plan.

It will never be possible to find inside of you the reasons why you were created, but only in the Creator. It is not about you, it is about Him, because at the end of the day He is the source, the origin, and the beginning of everything. *"You can make many plans, but the Lord's purpose will prevail"* (Proverbs 19:21 NLT). I would not be talking to you about purpose if I was not seeking for its origin myself, and I have understood that everything revolves around Him – this book will not be the exception.

These pages narrate God's unquestionable persistence in showing us His plan, in training us to understand His purpose and walk in it, and they describe the valuable tools with which we, in our humble condition, have been equipped so that we can reflect Him to the world.

When reading this book, you will also find valuable additional teachings and stories about specific moments in my childhood, teenage years, and adulthood, where things are not always seen from the best angle.

But before you dive right into the content of these chapters, I must explain to you that many of the decisions that I made in the past are a consequence of the way of thinking that I had then. If your ideas feel confronted by any statement made in this book, you are free to hold onto what is good and follow up your read with the beautiful and perfect guide of the Holy Spirit.

I will tell you in advance that the Father inspired every word in the writing process of *God has a purpose with you* and I also looked for the guidance of people who love and fear the Lord, surrounding myself with wise advice to write what would be most convenient and edifying for you at the moment of reading it.

After reading some pages, I hope you allow me the confidence of your friendship, as I will need it so that every one of my words is sowed into you as a seed in good soil that will produce many fruits. I have been praying for you before you were able to hold this book in your hands, and that is why I am confident that it will be a tool that will strengthen your spiritual life and will reveal the importance of a life in constant communion with the Father.

Although you will find my life story in these chapters, I urge you not to get distracted with the events, thoughts, and situations I have experienced in my past, as this book was not conceived with the intention of being another self-help book based on the human heart. I have only used some of my life experiences as the starting point that will help me explain the real reason **why** God blew His breath on me, with the only intention of allowing His glorious intervention to be seen in my insignificant circumstances. *"And we know that all things work together for good to them that love God, to them who are the called according to his purpose"* (Romans 8:28 KJV).

In this book, I have compressed everything that I consider could contribute, encourage, and nurture those who have a calling and ministry but still have many questions to have a clear understanding of how and where they can serve God.

This is my gift to you: ten chapters packed with teachings; consider them like a pair of shoes you can wear until you start feeling deep inside of you there´s a resemblance with your daily life. And if you happen to experience brokenness, happiness, confrontation, love, and any other bittersweet feeling while reading this book, I'm not responsible for that, as by then you will have noticed that God is hidden behind these letters, longing to speak to you with intensity, exposing His burning desire to draw you closer to Him, and destroying every lie that the enemy has ever said about you - for above all else *God has a purpose with you,* and this is the moment to discover it.

Robert Green

AN UPSIDE-DOWN HOUSE

Chapter 1

Chapter 1

AN UPSIDE-DOWN HOUSE

JUST LIKE IN EVERY GOOD FICTION STORY, there must always be heroes and villains. Growing up, we used to read comics where villains were defeated, and heroes cheered. Since we were little, we wanted to pretend we were heroes, those who save the lady from falling into the void. But nobody wants to be the villain, the one who plans destructive strategies to make everybody else suffer.

You might try to find heroes and villains in this story I will now tell you, and you will find men and women, just like you and me, who are constantly making choices – some of them good, others not – but who are loved and forgiven by God, because they are His beloved sons and daughters.

But at what moment does God decide that we can make our appearance on earth, and who will be the family that will embrace us? Although we do not know this, we are convinced that His decisions are perfect. So, I recognize His great goodness by allowing me having been born in a great family. For me, the best one there is.

Dominican Republic is the nation where my parents, my two sisters and I were born. Together, we created a home where God had, without doubt, the most important place. We were a pastoral family, and for that reason most of our time was spent inside the church, which I consider to be one of the greatest gifts God could have given me.

My father, Ramón Green, was the pastor of the church. Being his son has shaped my destiny and purpose in my journey with God in a very positive way. My father's figure was, and still is, the closest inspiration to imitate the lifestyle of someone who loves the Lord with his whole heart.

I have always related my story to the story of Samuel the prophet. Since the moment I was born, I was set apart and dedicated to the Lord and the service of His house. Being the pastor's son does not guarantee a special closeness to God, but the responsibility of growing a personal relationship with Him. However, I must admit that there are very valuable teachings that come with the benefits of counting with a constant pastoral coverage and the limitations one must comply with regarding behavior for being part of the pastoral family.

THE INFLUENCE OF THE WORD

Since my childhood, the seed of the living Word was sown in my heart and even if in that moment I did not understand it all, years later I was able to see the fruit of everything I had learned during my early days.

My father, Ramón, and my mother, María, had taken a commitment to guide their children in the way of salvation, taking Proverbs 22:6 as their own: *"Train up a child in the way he should go: and when he is old, he will not depart from it."*

Both my sisters and I have been refined, preserved, and disciplined as beloved children to become men and women planted in our faith. I have learned from my own experience the importance of instructing our kids at home and at church. No matter how mischievous they could be sometimes, as it is something natural in them, the lessons that we learn guide us to grow and develop God's purpose in our life. The Bible says: *"Let the little children come to me, and do not hinder them, for the kingdom of heaven belongs to such as these"* (Matthew 19:13-15 NIV).

I am still moved to tears whenever I remember the moments, we used to gather in our living room to pray and read the Word of God together as a family. Each morning, alongside with my family, I had my first experiences of praise and worship in the simplicity of our home. That is one of the best stages I have ever set foot in. It is where I learned the value and the importance of intimacy with the Lord.

Every morning at the beginning of the day, before school or work, my dad would wake my sisters Catherine, Caroline, and I at 5:45 AM singing with his powerful voice: *"Christ is coming, there are signs, He´s coming to seek saved souls, those who are asleep will stay, but those who stayed awake will come with Him."*

Can you imagine waking up kids from ages 3 to 7 in such a way? It was not fun at all! Every time that I, still asleep, would hear the phrase "those who are asleep will stay", I jumped out of my bed in a hurry to join the family service. Now that I think about it, these were the first manifestations of fear of the Lord that I had in my life.

We had to prepare songs for Him every day. That is how I learned, with my parents' help, that worship is not about us, and the goal is not to collect personal accomplishments, but to please the Lord. My personal and spiritual development emerged amid all these moments, and it was there that I discovered music, with my hands and my voice as my best instruments. I remember how everyone went crazy whenever I sang in the stairs, because of the great acoustic in our two-story house. But even when I was being too loud, they gave me a lot of grace as I was, without any doubt, passionate about music.

All these experiences led me to acquiring the habit of singing between the ages of 8 and 11 and although I did not have any studies in this beautiful art, I loved singing and I was able to recognize the power there is in worship and how God used it to move. I worked hard to learn and improve my talent so that I could worship the Lord with my voice.

I never imagined this would finally be my ministry, let alone receive a contribution for it. I was just focused on giving my best to please God's heart through my voice and my worship. I was extremely grateful for His faithfulness and the sacrifice He had made for me first.

THE PRESSURE THAT COMES WITH PRIESTHOOD

My childhood was well-founded in God. However, growing up in church with my parents as the pastors, I experienced some struggles that probably resulted from me being in that place. At church I learned about the great commitment pastors make through their total surrender, although many fail to respond to that sacrifice the right way. Being close enough to see the beautiful service of my parents taught me to always give my best. It was not always pleasant - that is why it is called a sacrifice – but in the end, God is always a better rewarder than men.

Although it is a great blessing, having been raised up in the hallways of the church had its complications. When you are the pastor's kid people expect a lot more from you than anybody else; all eyes are on you, everyone in the congregation knows who you are, and they have high expectations of you. That pressure made me think that I did not have the right to fail.

That meant that not only was my family looking out for me, but also the whole church watched my steps closely. With time, God helped me to not be affected by all of it and not to concentrate too much on what others were saying or doing and focusing my heart on serving the Lord and loving and serving my neighbors.

As ministers, my parents had more pressure and responsibility of keeping their house in order than any other family. It is not only cultural; the Bible also categorizes the pastoral family as a model, one to be imitated. It felt like a great pressure for us but also for our parents, who had different perspectives one from the other regarding certain things. This brought some problems at home, for my mother began visiting other churches, identifying with certain forms she considered closer to her own way of thinking, in contrast to my father, who had complete opposite concepts about how a Christian should live.

Despite the so characteristic maturity and wisdom my parents carried, little by little my "exemplary" home began taking a new direction, until we found ourselves in one of the hardest processes I had to experience in my childhood. The enemy took advantage of that situation to wear down everything we had built with so much love and sacrifice through the years.

Both my parents were so firm in their own opinions that it had begun to fracture the harmony in our home. Some were generated by the high standards we had to comply with, and even if we wore a mask with our best smile to church, the circumstances at home were really tough.

At first, my dad was trying to defend "God's ways" by not allowing women to wear pants or specific make up products even at home. On the other hand, my mother believed none of these things offended the Lord and, in that moment, my father was not able to understand it. The different opinions created a great division, placing me between two opposite thoughts about how a Christian should be. And even if the church was built outside our home, inside of it, it was collapsing.

My father was so determined to defend God that we also experienced him play the role of a pastor in our house, and his radical way of thinking against the "contemporary ways" could not be ques-tioned. For us it was not easy – he was not only our father, but he was also our pastor. Usually, if you have any problem at home you go to your pastor or leader to seek help and advice. And if you have a problem at church, you talk about it with your dad at home. But in my case, both were the same person.

If there is one thing I am completely sure about, is the love my father has for the Lord. His passion in guiding us through the right path made him become radical before any situation that could harm us or make us divert from God's purpose. He dreamed of having a perfect family that would be a role model for others, and he was determined to go against anything that could get in his way to achieve it. As a good father, he protected us and set us apart for the Lord, but the tenacity of his arguments made the situation more and more complicated.

"THE BEST GUIDE
CAN ONLY COME FROM ONE
EXCLUSIVE HEAD: CHRIST!"

AN UPSIDE-DOWN HOUSE

All these different concepts and confusions made the administration of the house problematic, and because of the roles each of them had and the lack of willingness to understand each other, the conflict got bigger. We endured, cried, and talked a lot, but we were in the middle of such a huge trial that therefore my mother moved away from home.

This filled my heart with sorrow, and even though I always hoped she would return, that never happened. A root of bitterness and anger began growing in my heart towards my father and God. As a kid, I needed to blame someone for what I was feeling. Years later I understood that neither God, nor my father or mother were responsible.

Yet, the void my mother left opened the door to many negative thoughts that made me see my heroes as the villains that had stolen what I loved most: my mom, who had always been the closest person to me.

She was no longer home but my sisters and I continued to live under my dad's commandments. The pain I was feeling for not having her living with us made me see my father through other eyes. Bitterness began filling my heart and I did many things to bother my father, with the only intention of hurting him. The admiration that I had was turning into a resentment that blinded me and did not let me see all those attributes I used to love about him.

My attitude and reactions got worse with every passing day, and I did not even leave my room to share a meal as a family. I would spend days without eating and I barely spoke with my dad unless it was necessary. My rebellion led me to stop going to church. My apathy, associated with resentment, pushed me into acting the way.

I respected and believed in God, but I began doubting his attributes of "Father", because I did not feel that closeness and paternity everyone always spoke about; I just felt a distant respect for Him. I understood He took care of me, but at the same time I felt He was ready to punish me if I made a mistake. That was my belief. The days kept going by and my emotional state was only drawing me further and further away from Him.

My dad had enough reasons to try to correct me due to my immaturity and defiance, but one afternoon, while we were having dinner, we got into a huge fight, and I saw no other option than to run (literally) to my mother's house. I returned a couple of days later, while my dad was gone, to pick up my clothes and moved out with my mom for good. This choice teared me away from my sisters - obviously from my dad as well – and brought an even bigger sense of emptiness to my life.

Now that I have children, I am totally aware that my father's intentions by trying to protect us from the things of the world were good and honest, but in that moment, I could not see what was going on in the spiritual realm; the only things I could concentrate on were my frustrations and wounds.

This story might place you either in the position of the father or the position of the son, and it might help you give God permission to heal your heart, just like He did with mine. I cannot help but tell you that now that I am a dad, I have learned that one must add prayer to words of authority, so that your family understands that biblical guidelines are sweeter than this world's trends.

With the years, I understood that there were not heroes nor villains in my story; that the only one and true enemy is the same one that creation has had since the beginning, the one who tried to ruin God's plan for families, which is: to educate their children in love so that their only priority would be to seek God's face.

To all of you men, householders, I remind you that you have the responsibility to exercise priesthood at home with love, wisdom, and self-control. Your obligation is that your house becomes the home that God and His family yearns for. Pleasing God is better than being funny with our kids and believing it is better to have an "upside-down house." We must have sensibility and patience to guide our dear ones with love.

Sharing this part of my story with you moves me one more time, because now, as an adult I understand the different circumstances that exposed my noble childlike heart to the pain of a family break up, and it brings me to reflect on a past where God was extremely present. He has always been there, in the mouths of those who surrounded me, in the songs that we used to sing in the living room, in the awe, praise and faith of the members of our church, but my wounded heart needed a personal encounter with Him. I needed to find "God's purpose for my life".

Let's reflect together

If by reading this chapter you have felt identified with your own life experiences – or it even brought back part of your story – I invite you to grab a piece of paper and write down the following:

1– Which were the moments of sorrow experienced in your childhood that have marked your heart? Express them in words.

2– What feelings were awakened while writing down your past experiences?

I invite you to go back to those memories that bring you so much pain and allow God to heal your sorrow and soothe your wounds with His hand of love. We can all comprehend – and even empathize – with your experiences, but God is the only one who can heal your emotions. Kneel, tell Him how you felt and ask Him to heal each one of your memories. I can assure you He is willing to heal your wounds so that those scars become a testimony in your life, just like they did in mine.

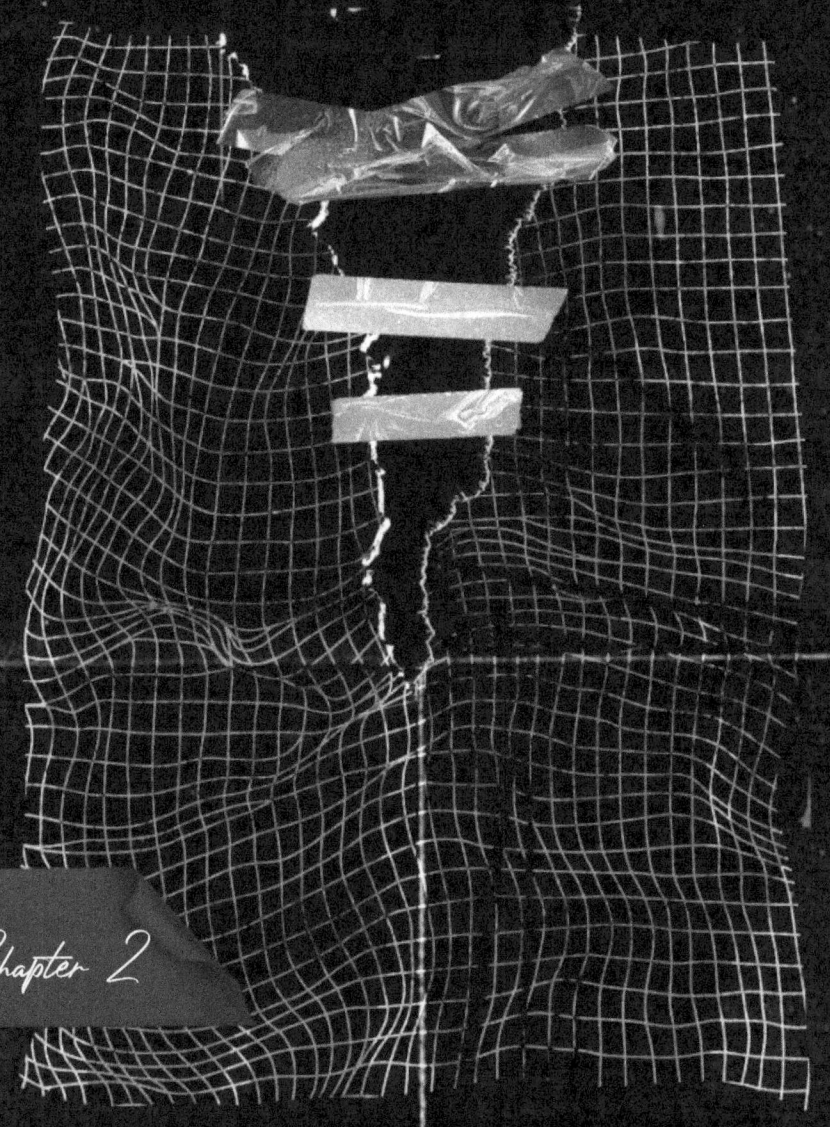

Chapter 2

THE FATHER'S
IMAGE

Chapter 2

THE FATHER'S IMAGE

RUNNING DOWN THE STREET; anger, pain and disappointment pushed me to go faster. My heart was pounding, a combination of mixed feelings. The adrenaline of what had happened, added to the tears clouding my vision made me run-away, as if I was escaping from a tragedy or a difficult situation. Even if I knew those were my last moments in that house, I did not have the chance to pick up my stuff or take a few minutes to say goodbye; I just had to get out of there.

As an impulsive teenager, after a fervent argument and some almost-yelled-words, I decided to humanly break the bond that I had with my father, along with a couple of dishes that I, acting out of anger, smashed against the floor of our kitchen. I walked away from my home's coverage and created an extremely painful fracture when I left a part of the wonderful team that we had put together since the day I was born, fourteen years prior to that day. The only thing that I proved with such attitude was that I was tearing down some areas of my soul and fracturing my obedience. Damaging the "father-son" bond that I valued so much caused me a lot of pain.

When I got to my mother's house, I was able to vent to her about everything that was going on in my mind and heart amid my anguish, tiredness, and pain. As days went by, those feelings of sadness, re-gret and fear were numbed by a comforting feeling of "freedom", which in a way made me think that everything would be fine, when in fact I had many wounds that needed healing.

I took the same decision that my mother had taken not so long before me and, just like her, I gradually began getting used to a new lifestyle - with a great difference: in my immature mind and transitional teenage stage I left open doors from the past that, in one way or another, brought consequences with time.

I made the decision of breaking the bond with my father, and over time I forgot what it felt like to have a father-son relationship, not only with my natural father but with my Heavenly Father as well. It is essential for a son to count with the protection, teachings, and love that a paternal coverage provides.

The need for a father that I naturally felt as a teenager contributed to the state of severe depression and loneliness that I plunged into, and although God and my father were always available to me, I did not dare to go to them. The deep wound motivated me to find someone I could put my trust in, and I decided to trust in myself. Despite having my mother around, my anger caused me to look away from God's purpose and lose my identity, for I did not have the supervision of a father or a pastor anymore, only that of a full-time working mother.

«IF THERE'S NO LOVE TO FORGIVE AND FORGET, WE'LL WALK AROUND BROKEN AND FULL OF WOUNDS TO HEAL.»

MY TALENT, MY PRIDE

Looking for something to hold on to, I became friends with my own talent. I discovered that I had singing skills, and this prompted me to give my best to improve those skills so that I could receive the admiration and praise that would fill the void in my heart.

My mother and I began attending a church near our house. I attended only to please her, but in that place, I found an opportunity to show my singing skills. The worship ministry would become the platform where I would surround myself with talented people who would help me learn more about vocalization. Without saying a word to anyone, motivated by a spot at the altar, I focused on practicing and searching online for everything related to singing. I downloaded audio editing software, bought a microphone, and used hundreds of Christian instrumental tracks to perfect my voice.

Naturally, these practices paid off, but at the same time I began feeling pride for the progress I was achieving thanks to my personal effort. Conscious that I had been able to improve with my own strength, I walked even further away from God, and I hit rock bottom by trying to boast about my skills. I write this with great shame but being completely honest so that you can understand the process I was going through.

o   The stage of rebellion that I was in, added to the resentment I carried inside and pushed me to do things that I knew were not right according to what I had learned at home. God always took care of me, and even though I never tried alcohol, used drugs, or had an unbridled lifestyle, the feelings in my heart diverted me from the future my parents had planned for me: to serve God with a pure heart every day of my life (like Samuel did).

I wasted a lot of time taking part in festivals, karaoke, and competing with some talented friends. I must clarify that I am saying this was a waste of time because in those days my goal was not to exalt the name of Jesus, but to take the glory to myself - a glory that did not belong to me at the time, does not belong to me now, and will never belong to me, since God is the only one worthy of all glory and honor.

I loved to sing high notes, that is, to considerably raise the pitch of a song, to cause a "wow" effect and impress anyone who heard me. With this attitude of believing I was able to compete and beat anyone, I auditioned for one of the most important TV programs, *Latin American Idol,* and I was selected as one of the ten finalists. I participated in a festival called *Mi voz para Cristo* [My voice for Christ], one of the most important catholic competitions in the country and won third place. I was also part of a festival called Buscando Adoradores 2006 [Seeking worshippers 2006], a contest held by the Conservative Evangelical Fellowship, where I got first place. As you may notice, I crossed religious barriers without minding beliefs - I was just motivated by the applause and praise I received.

God tried to speak to me many times amid my rebellion, but I would not listen to Him. Until one day, in His persistent desire of drawing me near to Him to show me the love of the Father, He went beyond my limits.

«GOD WANTS TO RESTORE
OUR PAST, BLESS OUR
PRESENT AND USE US IN
THE FUTURE.»

A DECLARED WORD

One afternoon, while trying to persuade my aunt, María Cristina, to help me sell tickets to the last festival's final, God saw the perfect opportunity to restore His image of Father and give me a taste of His Presence in a prophetic language that would make me realize that He was with me. Unexpectedly, with the tickets in her hand and filled with God's authority, my aunt said, "You'll compete, and you will win first place, but it'll be taken away from you. God will then give it back to you, and if you honor Him alone, there won't be another voice like yours in the Dominican Republic". My disconnected heart did not understand it, but I looked her in the eyes and hesitantly said: "I believe it".

The day and time for the grand final came and I was very excited. The auditorium was packed with a large audience. After several hours where we all sang, they were finally going to announce the positions of the six winners. I was biting my nails; the jury had its verdict. They had medals, trophies, and plaques in their hands, and with great enthusiasm and a radio announcer voice, the host announced each position. After calling the first two participants, they called out my name to give me the third place, and as I was already holding the plaque in my hands, the jury suddenly decided to relocate the positions of the six winners. When I heard this, my heart began racing, as I remembered the prophecy my aunt had given me and I remained in that tense atmosphere, expectant of what was going to happen in the few minutes that followed. Sure enough, God fulfilled His word by giving me first place.

I was overjoyed with my achievement, but most of the audience wasn't, so many were booing and shouting, "Fraud! Fraud!". Leaving me as a cheater in front of everyone.

God showed up in the story proving me that He had control over everything, and that He was giving me a chance to recognize that it was all about His grace and favor. That my accomplishments and triumphs were not a guarantee of people's support and admiration. God was thoroughly trying to make me understand what I could achieve if I chose to honor Him and the way I could keep on living if I did not accept my calling. I was supposed to feel satisfaction for this achievement, but that inconvenient outcome touched my heart in the least expected way.

Even after this experience, my rebellion did not cease; I continued swimming upstream. From that moment on, it seemed as if someone was thwarting my incessant search for recognition. People would ask me, "Robert, have you recorded your album yet? When's the release?". So, my answer was, "We're getting close, not long now", but the truth was that since that moment, everything began to go wrong. I never got the prize that I won at the contest: to record an album. It seemed as if someone was taking away from me every opportunity, cornering me.

With time, life became more and more difficult to me, and as I grew older, I began feeling the need to generate income to help with the everyday expenses at home. All my effort had been poured into singing. I sang at weddings, birthday parties and even at churches where I would get a compensation, but the truth is that the money I was receiving was not enough compared to the effort I was investing into it.

There was too much pressure generated by the people around me; those who knew what was going on would suggest me to start investing my time in something that would really provide to me financially since, apparently, my efforts for accomplishing something big with my talent did not make any sense.

"I'M YOUR FATHER"

I quit music and began transcribing documents for a living. My days were packed with work and my nights filled with tears from the extreme depression and frustration I felt by seeing myself as a total loser. Questions yelling inside of me, "Why? Why does it happen to other people and not me? What is wrong with me? What am I doing wrong?"

I had no more reasons to get out of such depression, for I felt my life was meaningless. The desire of running aimlessly came back when I hit rock bottom, the same one I felt the day I run away from home. I stopped trusting myself and, what is worse, I felt like my life had no purpose.

It was with great disappointment that I decided to run away again, to get as far as I could from my home. But as I ran, with the possibility of opting for death, I suddenly felt as if someone stood in my way, and I was stopped by the impact of a warm, enveloping hug that left me breathless. And I heard God's wonderful voice that said, "I'm your Father."

My senses faded immediately and with a powerful cry I felt how those words pierced the deepest part of my soul. It was such a supernatural love that I could not resist it - all I could do was to get lost in His arms. In my brokenness, I made the most sincere prayer I had ever made. I confessed how much I needed God and how sorry I was for my mistakes. So, God began His restoration work, allowing me to meet Him one more time to understand, heal and give an end to the orphanhood I had embraced since the moment I walked away from my earthly father.

The moment I humbled myself as a repentant son, I understood that He was not only aware of my flaws or the things that went wrong in my life to punish me, but that He could, and wanted to, restore, and love me even with my worst mistakes.

I reflected on how far I had run from home and how many times I rejected, like a prodigal son, the accessible grace of my Father, who had always been available to me and how I, in my apathy, lived so distant from the One who was relentlessly trying to restore His image of a Father in my heart.

He freed me from my bondage and adopted me again as His son with His strong embrace.

"The Spirit you received does not make you slaves, so that you live in fear again; rather, the Spirit you received brought about your adoption to sonship. And by him we cry, "Abba, Father." (Romans 8:15 NIV)

That is our true identity - we are His sons and daughters, He is our Father, and He loves us unconditionally. A father's first virtue is love. A father suffers for his children and disciplines them; not to mistreat them but to guide them to the best outcome, not allowing the vanities of this world to distract them.

His love is endless. His love is persistent. His love pursues us. His love goes after us, even in the worst storm. The Bible says: "And after my skin has been destroyed, yet in my flesh I will see God" (Job 19:26 NIV). That is, when you have reached the lowest point from the human condition, the Lord will raise you from the dust.

Knowing God is like when you meet a new friend. At first there's not enough trust, but with time the relationship gets stronger. I remember that at first my prayers were short because I did not want to tell him much - I was still afraid He would judge or reject me - so I began praying short prayers, saying, "Good night, I ask You to protect me, and I want You to know that I love You".

The words that led me to be unknown to the world but a close friend to God were few but meaningful. And by humbling my soul, I began to experience the most beautiful days of restoration, rebuilding and redirection that saved my destiny from failure, and even from death.

My conversations with God increased gradually, up to the point of spending entire nights talking with Him. Even sometimes I was on the street, and I felt the urge of getting home to spend time with the Lord. It was amazing to be reunited with the God I had met in my childhood, with the only difference that now there was a greater and more intense personal contact. I was happy to be by His side. How beautiful it was to delight myself in His Presence, to feel the Holy Spirit's embrace without any fear of acknowledging my weaknesses. Just like a surgery in an operating room, God was removing my weaknesses and tuning my heart according to His will. I was not afraid, because I knew the doctor was my friend.

The Lord tells us to come to Him with our burdens and He will give us rest (Matthew 11:28). Those burdens are sins, disappointments, wounds, resentments, things that the pastor and your family dislike, but Christ tells you to give Him the weight of that burden you are carrying, promising to ease the weight on your shoulders and give you rest.

I must admit that my biggest burdens where those that I had chosen to carry resentment, ego, and bitterness from failure. These are so heavy that I would not recommend anyone to carry them.

FORGIVENESS AND RESTORATION

As I gave myself permission to develop an intimate relationship with my Heavenly Father, He dealt with modifying the last image I was dragging of my earthly father. As soon as I began forgiving myself and healing my wounds, as a prodigal son, I was able to victoriously restore the relationship with my dad and pastor.

After ten years, I asked him to forgive me. And I found out that, because of his unconditional love, he had been waiting for me with open arms since the first day I left. Our friendship began growing gradually, and we became best friends by letting go of our painful past. Since that moment, I value the many virtues that I loved and still love about him.

It is amazing what can happen when we change the religious paradigm of respecting God for the consequences it may bring, to a fear that is purely moved by love and by how kind He is to us. That intimate relationship leads us to honor and not fear.

We can open the door of our heart to God for Him to enter as a stranger, and He will manage to become a friend, a lover, a husband, a Father. We just need to let it clear that we yearn for a relationship with Him.

God has restored the lives of thieves, homosexuals, drug addicts and alcoholics, among others. In my case, He straightened my path by trading my frustrations for the joy of His salvation (Psalm 51:12).

The God we must learn to know is the One who has purpose in our life, who longs to restore us, who, like an instrumentalist, is ready to bring the best sound out of us by tuning us, cleaning us, taking care of us, and improving what is wrong for our good. That is His unconditional love. He wants us to work with Him based on our personal relationship and not through others' experiences.

My father's image was completely restored and with it, I recovered my identity as a son. I was finally able to get rid of my ego, my dreams, and personal plans, and begin searching for the real purpose for which I was called. When I learned to hear God's voice, His will became irresistible to me and I completely forgot about my own desires - I became fully passionate about His.

Everything seemed to be taking the perfect course. Then I realized how much time I had wasted on myself, which caused in me a desire to diligently do everything in my power to accelerate and execute His plan in my life. I understood it was impossible to do it alone, so I asked God, "How am I going to do this?" And He replied: "With the gifts and talents that I have given you".

Perhaps you have gone through a similar experience, and my story reveals your spiritual reality. You must still know that God has many gifts ready to give you. Let us continue this journey together and you will discover the gifts He has also prepared for you.

Let's reflect together

The pain and sorrow brought by my mother moving away from home caused me not only grief, but rebellion and lack of forgiveness. Therefore, I walked away from God's purpose for my life:

1– *Have you entertained feelings of resentment towards those who have hurt you?*

2– *Have you allowed rebellion to control your life and guide you through paths you now understand are not the right ones?*

3– *Have you ever experienced the uncertainty of not knowing who to turn to? Has frustration made you feel as if God was not going to have you back as His son?*

4– *Do you need to forgive someone or heal a wound from the past?*

Feelings of resentment, hate, or lack of forgiveness are bondages that do not allow you to move forward and keep you in unproductive places. God's plans are the only ones that lead you to the destiny that will guide you to the purpose for which you were called. As an act of courage and with great conviction, forgive the person who has hurt you. Ask God to forgive you for having given rebellion a place in your heart and confess your mistakes to Him. He is the One who forgives all our sins and frees us from the curse that comes from resentment and rebellion. He restores our identity as sons and daughters.

Chapter 3

THE GIFTS GOD HAS GIVEN ME

Chapter 3

THE GIFTS GOD HAS GIVEN ME

WHEN I RETURNED TO GOD and began trying to make the most of the time I had wasted, I discovered things about Him that I did not know before. I became passionate about making Him known to everyone, but I understood that in addition to His grace I was going to need tools to equip me to fulfill the universal purpose: to "go and make disciples of all nations, teaching them to obey everything He has commanded us" (Matthew 28:19-20); as well as discovering the individual call that Christ made to every believer.

I must admit that I was not good at math when I was in school. No matter how much I studied, my grades were very low, so I always had to ask a classmate who was able to quickly understand the teacher's explanations for help. It was obvious that I was not talented with numbers, but that did not mean I did not have talents at all.

You might have heard of Pablo Picasso or Leonardo Da Vinci, famous artists known for their painting skills. That was the talent God placed in them as artists and they used it to create pieces of art that marked history around the world. Without doubt, they were born for that.

However, talents are not always used for the benefit of the Kingdom of heaven. God created us with natural capacities to serve one another, even if man makes use of these for different activities.

There are countless virtuous people, such as musicians, doctors, physicists, engineers, actors - among others - who are celebrated for their skills. Regardless of whether they are Christians or not, God has blessed them with wonderful talents. Despite the merit they have obtained individually for perfecting their skills, studying, and acquiring more knowledge on the subject, without God, it is not possible to completely fulfill the goal they were designed for, since they will never be able to achieve the purpose for which they were called.

GIFTS AND TALENTS

As children of God, we limit ourselves by not knowing the abilities, skills, and strengths that the Lord has given us out of His great love. His Word calls these gifts and talents. And they are both defined as follows:

- Gift: manifestation of God's power given to believers for service.

- Talent: a special intellectual aptitude or skill that a person learns easily or at great capacity to develop an activity.

When understanding these concepts there is a question that comes to mind, one that I've asked myself and it's probable you have done it too: "Are there any talents and gifts in me? Which are they?"

We could define talents as natural or innate abilities, for example: an inner ear for music, an ability to serve others, charisma for leadership or a vocation to a particular occupation. On the other hand, gifts are supernatural abilities, such as prophecy, healing, faith, among others. Those gifts given by God, added to our talents, are tools used to raise and build the Kingdom of God on the Earth.

1 Peter 4:10 says: "As each one has received a special gift, employ it in serving one another as good stewards of the multifaceted grace of God" (NASB).

The words "each one" and "special gift" call my attention, for I understand that God - in His generosity - gave special, unique, and authentic gifts to each person individually. However, this verse specifies the gifts of service referred to in Romans 12:

"We have different gifts, according to the grace given to each of us. If your gift is prophesying, then prophesy in accordance with your faith; if it is serving, then serve; if it is teaching, then teach; if it is to encourage, then give encouragement; if it is giving, then give generously; if it is to lead, do it diligently; if it is to show mercy, do it cheerfully" (verses 6-8 NIV).

These are different to the gifts described in 1 Corinthians 12, which are the ones received after the fullness of the Holy Spirit: "Now to each one the manifestation of the Spirit is given for the common good. To one there is given through the Spirit a message of wisdom, to another a message of knowledge by means of the same Spirit, to another faith by the same Spirit, to another gifts of healing by that one Spirit, to another miraculous powers, to another prophecy, to another distinguishing between spirits, to another speaking in different kinds of tongues, and to still another the interpretation of tongues. All these are the work of one and the same Spirit, and he distributes them to each one, just as he determines" (verses 7-11 NIV).

It is amazing to know the different gifts that God made available to us, and because of this, I encourage you to study them in detail, for I know that the Holy Spirit will use it to help you discover everything that He has already given to you and what He still wants to give you.

PERSEVERANCE

We are not always able to recognize at first sight the gifts and talents God has given us; in my personal case, I asked myself many questions before discovering them. Although I used to sing in my house from a very young age, whenever my dad asked us to sing a song, if I had to compare myself to my sisters, I was not the one who did it best due to my shyness.

Ever since I was a little boy, I had hangups about my voice, and I was terrified of speaking in public. At that time, I was attracted to singing but I was not the best at it; so, I chose to be the funniest person of the group to somehow lose my shyness and call other peoples' attention.

This ended in my teenage years, when my mother confronted me with her words, "Robert, if you like to sing, don't belittle what God has given you and don't try to hide it behind jokes. Improve the talent that has been given to you, get the best out of it. If you have the will to be passionate about what you really want to do, our Lord will use your character and your weaknesses to be glorified and you will learn how to sing well. God will still do it through your shyness, and if you reject your distinctive attributes and who you are, you are actually rejecting the gifts and talents God has given you".

These words just came alive inside of me. And from that moment on, I began working hard. I was not good from the beginning, but I got interested in music and I put all my effort in growing my talent.

There was a church near my house that caught my attention because every time I walked by, I saw young people singing a capella. As I saw them practice every day, an intriguing interest for knowing them grew inside of me. With great shyness I began approaching them gradually, until I met one of the members of the group, who kindly introduced me to the rest of them.

I greeted them and since that day I began attending their rehearsals every afternoon. I had found people who loved the same thing I did. I became friends with each of them to learn from them all, because I had great interest in developing the talent God had gifted me and that I was so passionate about.

They sang beautifully and sounded great when performing with a background track a song entitled "Golgotha" from the duet *Israel y Moisés*. I noticed how the leader of the group poured passion into the lyrics and I began dreaming with one day being able to sing like them. After I heard them sing, and with no hesitation, I complimented them for their singing and, in my shyness, I asked the leader of the group if he could give me the track of that song. I began practicing at home with that wonderful melody.

I remember that my practice hours were very demanding and for hours I tried to perfect myself more and more. I longed that, some day, when they heard me sing, these friends of mine would give me the chance to join the band. Every day on my way to rehearsals, I looked up, closed my eyes, and prayed to God, "Lord, make them ask me to sing with them today".

DON'T GIVE UP

When the choir began its practices that included singing such beautiful harmonies, I would get so excited that I could not remain silent and sang from afar, with the intention of being heard by the leader and asked to join them; but the only thing I accomplished whenever I did this, was that they would stop singing and ask me to shut up because it hindered what they were doing.

Anyone would have gotten offended if they were treated that way, but my passion for singing was stronger than my pride, and for that reason I worked even harder on perfecting my performance. This caused my talent to keep improving little by little.

I understood that despite being rejected, I could not give up what I was passionate about, and that it was my responsibility to prove that I could be good enough to be part of the band. It is our duty to develop and steward our talents in the best way possible, and when God sees that we are passionate and we do it well, He multiplies His grace over what He has given us.

According to the Parable of the Talents, a man distributed different amounts of talents among his servants for them to multiply them (Matthew 25:14-30). That is how I learned that God (alluding to the man in the parable) gave me talents as His servant, so that I could work hard and prove to Him how much I valued His gifts by multiplying them. You have a responsibility to do the same thing with what you have received.

It was very rewarding when, after some time, the guys from the band got surprised with how much I had grown in my singing, and I gave glory to God for it. I know that fervent desire that was within me to do things with excellence to please God was what made the Father pour His grace over what I did.

I could feel God backing me up in every place I visited. When I sang, the Holy Spirit made me say things that I was not even thinking. Those prophetic words were expressions of what God was activating in me; it was more than just talent; He was adding gifts that were quenched by my shyness and lack of diligence.

Talent and passion alone are worth nothing. Discipline applied to things where there is no talent or passion will take you nowhere. Talent, passion, and discipline need to be combined to serve others, but most importantly, the Holy Spirit's support is what causes God's purpose to reach us.

TALENT VS. CALLING

My advice is that you get over rejection and overcome shame, for they slow you down and do not allow you to receive a word from God to move forward. Just as the motivation I received from my mother - that awakened the potential that the Father had placed in me - I now tell you there are gifts and talents that God gave you and are still to manifest - you just need to develop them. No matter how small the beginning is, what others may say, or the limitations your shyness may bring you, God chose you as an important piece of His body and gave you talents; not for you to bury them out of fear of what others may say, but for you to boldly dare to serve others with the skills He placed in you.

Dare to dream. Dream as much as you want, if those dreams go hand in hand with what you know how to do well. That talent, if put for the service of God, will activate the gifts, and that gift will generate grace and favor that will make others get to know the Lord.

Keep dreaming with developing the gifts and talents He has placed in you, but be careful not to focus on them excessively, leaving aside the will of the One who has given them to you. I know that we have all been taught from a young age to fight for what we want. We get motivated at youth conferences and churches to work hard and diligently until we achieve our goals. But I will say something that will sound completely opposite to it, and that is: Don't focus too much on your dreams, because when we cling to them without taking God's will into account, we can be wrong about what we have chosen, according to our own judgement.

How many times as kids have, we dreamt of being astronauts, firefighters, policemen, or some kind of superhero? These might be dreams that we had because we were influenced by the TV. However, when we got to a certain age, we realized that we were wrong and said, "A superhero? An astronaut? These are not the dreams that I want for my life".

Later, in our teenage years, we probably wished to be singers or TV stars and we clung to that, not because of God's purpose, but because we wanted to follow the example of our favorite artist. Years later we said, "This is what I want to do for the rest of my life", without understanding that perhaps it was not even within the father's plan.

I have met people that want to sing and invest many years of their lives taking classes and exercising a ministry with music, hoping to fulfill "their dream", yet they are never fully satisfied, nor see the fruits of their discipline, for they have not asked God if these are the desires of His heart. Then you ask yourself, "Why is this happening to them?" My answer is the following:

"Those dreams were a distraction that kept them from striving in the activities for which God actually gave them talents". I used to ask myself, "Has God given me any talents? And if He has, which are they?"

Our talent or gift is not our calling. Above all things, our main calling is to love God, have a close relationship with Him and obey

His commandments. When we do this, serving - and using our abilities to do it - is a consequence of our love for Him. Some people misunderstood "being" with "doing" and think that they are closer to God by doing things with their gifts and talents, but it is not about what we do, it is about what we are when we are in intimacy with Him.

When dreams come from God, they are not selfish, they do not only bring personal gratification, and they are definitely not dreaming that one wishes to accomplish for a trend or fashion. With all our heart and effort, we must place in God's hands the known and hidden abilities that He has given us with the only purpose of developing them for His glory and honor. And ask the Father with humbleness and willingness of heart, "How can I serve You?" I can assure you He'll show you where and how you need to serve Him. Once you have the answer, lean on the love and passion you have for Him to improve and serve Him with the utmost excellence.

When I learned this, my life changed, and I began to see different results in my efforts. I noticed that my dreams were not actually "my dreams", but God's dreams manifested in me through the talents and gifts that He had given me.

God will not consider people who are focused on their own merits or passionate about their own abilities for the fulfillment of His dreams; He'll choose those who are wholeheartedly willing to grow the gifts and talents the Father has given them for His own glory.

Although our capacities, vocations, dreams, and wishes are useful and very important to God, they are perishable and temporary on this earth. The Holy Spirit gives meaning to what we do and a reason of why we do it. Follow me in my story and let us talk about the importance of having a constant and continuous relationship with the Holy Spirit.

Let's reflect together

Many think that gifts and talents are the same thing, but as we have read in this chapter, they are not. If we met today to talk and I asked you the following questions, what would you answer me?

1- Can you clearly identify the difference between gifts and talents?

2- Which are the talents that stand out in you, and which are the gifts God has given you?

To begin walking towards the purpose God has given you, it is very important you can identify your gifts and talents, as He'll use them for His purpose. If you do not know them, you will likely try to be someone you are not. Also, do not try to develop a gift that has not been given to you, because it is very probable, you will fail. Strengthen and grow what God has already determined for your life and I can assure you that you will fulfill the call He has placed upon you. Pray and ask God to help you discover what He has placed in your life.

INTIMACY WITH
THE HOLY SPIRIT

Chapter 4

THE *Holy Spirit* IS A GENTLEMAN, HE ONLY ENTERS WHERE HE IS WELCOMED.

Chapter 4

INTIMACY WITH THE HOLY SPIRIT

ONE OF THE MOST SIGNIFICANT VICTORIES of my life took place when at just 21 years of age I restored my relationship with my heavenly Father. This put an end to the depression that had conquered my mind when I tried and with my own strength to become a well-known singer, without considering the plan God had for my life.

After several months of walking through a restoration process, I arrived at *Tabernacle of Worship Church*. Shortly after that, and at the request of my pastors Santiago and Norelis Ponciano, I began serving as a musician at the altar, wholeheartedly interpreting the worship songs that would gradually help me discover what God had in mind from that moment onward.

During my first steps serving at the altar, I was able to feel when the Holy Spirit was present in the room, but it was not something that happened constantly. I sang many times because I knew how to, and I used the grace that the Lord had placed under my administration. Although my focus was not always the right one, God was still faithful to me in pouring His gifts, even when I did not feel the fullness of His fire burning inside of me whenever I praised Him.

However, something changed. As I deepened my relationship with Him and sought Him with intensity and a humble heart, unusual things began to happen every time that I ministered. For example, I would cry with no explanation whenever I sang, my whole body would shake, and I would feel God's presence very strongly upon me. On some occasions I even resisted it thinking it was more of an emotional thing rather than a spiritual one. And with my eyes closed I would try to calm myself down, afraid, and ashamed of what others might think of me.

After that amazing encounter I had had with the Father while I was running, the fear for God's presence, reverence, and respect for what He meant to me grew stronger. I was very expectant for what God wanted to do with me, but I knew that to complete His plan I needed a deeper experience with the Holy Spirit.

I attended every church service with a lot of enthusiasm, I sang in the choir, I saw and heard among the people the angelic tongues that declared all kinds of blessings for those who were present and warned about the presence of the Holy Spirit in that place, but in my case, I did not feel anything.

The gift of having an encounter to fully know Him, still hadn't manifested itself in my life and, apparently, God was preparing the perfect moment while He was working in my heart through a process based on seeking His face and waiting for that very special moment.

> "OUR RELATIONSHIP WITH THE HOLY SPIRIT MUST GROW EVERY DAY, NOT JUST TO RESPECT AND HONOR HIM, BUT TO LOVE HIM AND SEEK HIM."

AN IMPORTANT APPOINTMENT

One Tuesday night, at one of our weekly services, something that would disrupt my senses and renew my whole being to completely transform it was about to take place. As part of the worship choir, and in unity with my brothers and sisters, we were crying and growing in intimacy with the Spirit while we praised. I could see a wonderful and beautiful manifestation of the Holy Spirit moving in the church. However, when I saw people on the floor moved by the Presence, I became uneasy and got on my knees with the intention of going unnoticed amid everything that was going on.

While still declaring beautiful things to the Lord, an unexpected public proposal was made, inviting me to have access to something that in my mind I considered to be completely different. The guest preacher pointed to the choir, which was composed by thirty-six people. I quickly sat down and tried to hide because I was terrified of being called to the front, but he raised his arm, pointed to the choir, and said: "that young man over there, come to the front". I looked around expecting to see somebody else. I could not believe he was talking to me. "Me?", I asked. "Yes, come to the front!", he replied.

I walked to the front, unwillingly, because I did not want him to manipulate me, so I said to myself, "I'm not going to fall". My desire was that whenever the Holy Spirit baptized me or I spoke in tongues it would be something natural and real, and not forced or faked. The preacher looked me in the eyes, and these were his first words, "If you call upon the Holy Spirit, He'll come".

I had seen in previous occasions how certain people would manipulate the moment in a subjective way, and my father had taught me that that was a very sacred moment to let myself get carried away by the excitement of someone else laying hands on me. However, the preacher looked me in the eyes without touching me, yelling, or forcing any emotion. He just repeated his words, "If you call upon the Holy Spirit, He'll come". So, I thought, "This is exactly what I've been so careful about, but I'll do it anyway, just to please him".

I began praying with great shyness, saying, "Come, come, come... Holy Spirit", just like the preacher had suggested me.

Despite my unwillingness, I began feeling an extraordinary power flooding my whole body which made me want to dance. It was amazing! I could feel His glorious manifestation smashing my paradigms. I no longer minded yelling in a loud voice with tears in my eyes, "Come, Holy Spirit". An atmosphere of complete freedom was surrounding me. I was sure this was not manipulation, but the Holy Spirit baptizing me with new tongues.

I felt an uncontrollable joy. I was dancing on the altar, moving my hands, and crying, until I wrapped myself on the curtain that decorated the wall. From the moment that I had that encounter with the Holy Spirit, I stopped putting obstacles in His way and limiting Him. I have never been the same since that day!

Imagine how surprised I was! I could not believe what had happened to me. Deep inside I was feeling the prejudice of being pushed by men, but He was still visiting me. When the Holy Spirit comes, He tears down our prejudices and does whatever He wants with us. He had prepared that amazing date for two. It was such a vivid experience! To be in His arms, going round and round; it was amazing!

Feeling His arms around me made me travel back in time to when I was little, and my father grabbed me by the arms and played with me making me fly in circles. It was an extreme feeling and, in a way, a little bit dangerous, but I liked it and, even though I was afraid of falling, I would look at my father's eyes and he would always tell me, "Don't be afraid, you're safe in my arms".

It was beautiful! I felt loved, desired, forgiven. I felt God's tight embrace, as if He had also been waiting for that special and tender moment. It was like a romantic movie, where a couple runs towards each other in slow motion to hug after ten years of not being together. That is the way I could describe that wonderful encounter with the Holy Spirit. A hug that I wished was endless; that I wished nothing could stop or separate me from Him - not even for a second.

When I got home, I ran to my room; I even forgot to have dinner. I did not sleep at all that night. I just laid on my bed and started crying on my pillow. For the first time in a very long time, I felt cherished. I stared at the ceiling of my room wondering, "What did I do to have such a privilege?" I closed my eyes and searched every scene in my mind to identify what I had done that day to catch His attention. I knew in that moment that my life was so important to the Holy spirit as He was to me.

> "THE HOLY SPIRIT IS STRENGTH, POWER, THE VOICE OF THE FATHER AND THE LOVE OF THE SON, A FRIEND FROM HEAVEN WHO ALWAYS WALKS WITH YOU."

MY BEST FRIEND

After the beautiful experience of having received the baptism of the Holy Spirit in my life, I could not stop looking for ways to please Him and seeing Him work in everything, from the smallest to the biggest things.

It may seem crazy but every day I went to the balcony and yelled to every walker passing by my house saying, "Be filled with the Holy Spirit", waiting to see His power in action, because I was so filled with the Spirit that I felt I could challenge Him to see something supernatural take place. Nothing ever happened, but I still felt Him so close that, even if my natural eyes could not see Him, I knew He was there with me.

I talked, cried, laughed, and sang with Him. I told Him my weaknesses and although I knew He was there with me in every moment, it felt nice to tell Him how I had felt during the day.

Reading the Bible became a different experience; it was more efficient now. He spoke to me directly through Scripture. I felt it was alive! I could finally understand in my own flesh the similarity between God and His Word, "Sharper than any double-edged sword" (Hebrews 4:12). That is what I literally felt in my body when I read what He had to tell me.

I did not want Him to ever leave my life. I knew that it was my responsibility to keep Him close and, to this day, I do all of this just to feel I am His best friend.

Having waited so long to feel the Holy Spirit was worth it. Even though I walked for many years without feeling His full manifestation, God had already placed it inside of me to take care of me and as a guaranteed seal for the fulfillment of His promises (Ephesians 1:13-14).

John 14:16-17 says: "And I will ask the Father, and he will give you another advocate to help you and be with you forever— the Spirit of truth. The world cannot accept him because it neither sees him nor knows him. But you know him, for he lives with you and will be in you" (NIV)

This verse became so real in my life that I realized I could not receive what I did not know, and I had been postponing what had always been accessible to me: the wonderful outpouring of the Holy Spirit.

How come it had always been in me and yet I had not felt it before? I can understand that He promised to be with us every day of our lives and He cannot break His word, but it is our duty to cause that relationship to grow and make sure that His manifestation is constant in us. We achieve this by calling Him and constantly letting Him know how much we need Him.

He is patient and waits for the precise moment when your heart is lit on fire by His presence. Many Christians know Him only by name. Some may have had the opportunity to feel Him close, others experienced Him like a rushing wind, but very few people dare to know Him as a friend or comforter. Perhaps you underestimated having a relationship with the Holy Spirit - I also did in the past; but I want you to understand that without Him, singing would only be singing, and talent would only be talent, yet His move in us is what gives true meaning to our walk with the Father and what activates our gifts for the fulfillment of His purpose.

HOW CAN I LISTEN TO THE HOLY SPIRIT?

Walking without the constant advice of the Holy Spirit who guides, comforts, and confronts you every second of the day could be really dangerous for your daily life, so I radically tell you that refusing His company makes us part of the carnal things of this world. "For the flesh desires what is contrary to the Spirit, and the Spirit what is contrary to the flesh. They are against each other, so that you are not to do whatever you want (Galatians 5:17 NIV). Therefore, if we reject His breath of life upon us, we might as well consider ourselves as dead.

If you allow Him to become one with you and your friendship grows, you can prepare yourself to do, see and feel things you have never imagined. You may wonder, how can I listen to the Holy Spirit? How can I receive Him?

Simply tell Him: "Come, Holy Spirit" at every moment, in every circumstance. Make Him part of the big and small decisions. Involve the Holy Spirit in everything regarding your life, and ask Him questions such as, "What clothes would You like me to wear?" What should I eat? What should I read? What should I study? What area of my life do You want to improve? What can I do to please You more and more? He will use any means available to make His words get to you. Whether through Scripture, a preacher, a TV program, a song, or even the voice of your own conscience.

It is Him who, with His perfect essence becomes a part of your daily life. Keeping Him close seems easy, but if we were used to the lack of closeness, we could make the mistake of not giving Him the place He deserves.

Let us not be those who know the Holy Spirit from afar and admire great men of God who have an actual relationship with Him;

I remind you that it is necessary for all of us to receive Him. God longs to connect with all His children, every day, all day long. It is amazing to see miracles, signs, and wonders, but that is no guarantee that we are having intimacy (spirit to spirit) where the perfect communion is strengthened.

The Holy Spirit should not be a stranger in our life. He lives in us and even knows our darkest thoughts; He is the ideal person to confide your biggest secrets, frustrations, disturbances, and all kinds of thoughts. He reveals the truth in those moments where you could be on the verge of making the worst decisions, He brings protection and security, leaving your past behind, supporting your present, and guarding your future.

When you decide to have a relationship with Him, you no longer need to plan dates to meet with Him, for He now becomes noticeable every second of your life. His love is irresistible and with a few conversations He'll become your most trusted friend, the one you talk to every night and stay awake with. He is the One you will never want to fail, for once you know Him, you will comprehend the sensitivity that characterizes Him and how easy it could be for the relationship to cool off if we make the wrong decisions. He is the Comforter, your Helper, the One who reveals to you the Father's desires, who gives you gifts and heals your afflictions. He is your best friend. He's God Himself.

The Holy Spirit is defined by so many things that a mere chapter in this book could not even give you a hint of everything that He is. Therefore, if you want to know Him to the fullest, you will have to seek His manifestation in your life, and once you have received it, you will have a commitment to keep that flame of love burning forever.

There are two parts in a relationship, and they both get to the agreement of taking care of it and keeping it alive. I must warn you;

He might light the flame in you if you attend the Sunday church service, but the only way to keep the fire burning until the following service is through your communion and constant pursuit.

This happened to me, but once I experimented it, it became very clear to me that I was no longer willing to wait years to feel His presence again. I recognized that it was better to fight against my own flesh and overcome it daily through my relationship with the Holy Spirit, than obeying my apathy and human impulses and neglect Him. Believe me when I say, there is nothing more unpleasant than walking without His Presence.

CONQUERING GOD'S HEART

"So, I say, let the Holy Spirit guide your lives. Then you will not be doing what your sinful nature craves. The sinful nature wants to do evil, which is just the opposite of what the Spirit wants. And the Spirit gives us desires that are the opposite of what the sinful nature desires. These two forces are constantly fighting each other" (Galatians 5:16-17 NLT).

This text gave me an excellent piece of advice, and it also helped me understand the internal struggles I was experiencing daily. Once I received the Holy Spirit in my heart, I had to learn (what I believed I already knew) how to conquer God's heart with my music ministry. This process included a huge discovery of maturity that took quite a long time.

My attitudes had changed. I no longer felt the need to exhibit what I possessed, because I knew the consequences of turning my back on the glory that the Creator deserves. Although I must admit that I felt my ego struggling daily with the constant sacrifice of worshiping the Lord, my attitude towards God changed progressively. I felt the strength to overcome the difficult times through prayer, and I also felt more authority and support whenever I had to minister. Several months later, the doors began to open in my favor, and I went from being a member of the choir to leading worship in church.

Dear reader, there are not tricks, recipes or steps to follow - according to human strategies - for God to use you. It is all about forgetting about we, living in constant communion and knowing Him intimately to see Him be glorified and manifested however He wants.

I insist, communion and intimacy with the Holy Spirit is a responsibility that you and I have, without looking at someone else's relationship, for that comparison will not benefit anyone. Each person individually must be committed to make sure that his cup is overflowing.

No one can bring you closer to God. Many can show Him to you, but you are the only one with the final decision to accept the challenge of becoming one with Him in intimacy. Your heart must be a constant altar of worship to God with a humble attitude, recognizing His lordship over your life, with the understanding that it is He who has redeemed you from sin and death.

Usually, during a moment of worship and outpouring of the Spirit it is quite common for apathy to prejudice us to receive what God has for us, and if we lose the focus, our immaturity leads us to think that we are not experiencing God's Presence due to the singer or preacher.

Blaming a singer for not singing the songs according to certain preferences or a preacher for saying things that do not fit to certain concepts, can create Christians that are dependent on men rather than Christ. It is vital to recognize that our responsibility, commitment, and daily desire revolves around exalting the Savior, no matter what surrounds us.

In the same way, each singer or preacher must consider the responsibility of entering the Presence without blaming the congregation for not yelling «amen» as loud as they would like to or reprimanding the drummer for not rolling the drums with the precision he had in mind.

Nothing must limit our desire to conquer God's heart through worship, for we must not forget that only Christ is enough to fulfill the purpose for which we were called, and it is He who makes our ministry have a positive impact and be a blessing to those around us.

The Holy Spirit's manifestation will not always go according to our culture. Sometimes we idealize certain gestures as evidence that He is working, as, for example: the pastor that screams while preaching, the musicians that try to show off their percussion skills, and the preacher that treads heavily on stage.

And although I've nothing against these practices, I believe that we should not considerate these as a reference to differentiate those who are filled with the Holy Spirit from those who are not. No matter how someone may act on stage, his secret life is the one that will determine the real endorsement God will use to transform lives.

CONSTANT COMMUNION

The Holy Spirit is a gentleman. He will only inhabit wherever He's welcome. He works when we give Him permission to do so and grows when we wane. The best thing I could do whenever I felt the Holy Spirit filling the house where we worshipped was to let Him be free, lead worship according to what He revealed to me, bow down, and recognize that He reigned above that and every other moment.

I understood that it was useless to believe I was too wise, prepared, and gifted, because the Lord works better in me when I have a humble and teachable spirit, considering my desire to be more like Him.

Jesus received the Holy Spirit, and many could witness with their eyes how the Spirit rested on Him in the form of a dove. The Scriptures describe the dove as a symbol of peace, meekness, and simplicity. And that is exactly what I received when the Holy Spirit rested on me. The peace that comes from knowing that He'll always be with me. The meekness that forced me to die to my own flesh so that the Spirit could grow in me daily, and the simplicity – the fact that by just saying "Come", He is able to touch every single cell of my body by pouring Himself with so much power and love all at the same time.

I felt so identified with the manifestation of the Spirit that I dare to say that from the moment He first filled my life, my steps were no longer the same, for I learned to walk with the subtlety of someone who walks with a dove perched on his shoulder. I now meditate every movement, decision, thought and action with utmost delicacy, with the only purpose of not letting any mistake make it fly away from me. This is my responsibility forever.

Would you dare take on the challenge of walking for the rest of your days discovering the power, peace, comfort, friendship, and beauty of the One who is longing to have a permanent connection with you?

Close the door of your room and sing to Him with all your might:

"Come, oh come, Holy Spirit, come".

Let's reflect together

The quest for the Holy Spirit has been one of the most significant experiences of my life, and I hope it gets to be yours too. The touch of His embrace brought a revolutionary change to my devotional life. Receiving the baptism of the Holy Spirit radically changed my spirituality, and it is from that experience that I encourage you to begin that same quest in your quiet time with the Lord.

1– Have you ever experienced the fullness of the Holy Spirit? Relive now that experience.

2– Do you long to receive what the Bible teaches in the book of Acts chapter 1 as the "Promise of the Holy Spirit"?

If you want to have a special and unique encounter with the Holy Spirit you just must ask for it; close the door of your room, look for the song Ven Espiritu Santo [Come Holy Spirit] by Barak, put the book aside for a few moments and make this song your prayer. Sing it out loud and ask for His outpouring over your life. God will work supernaturally over you and you will never forget such an experience. Remember: "If you call upon the Holy Spirit, He'll come".

¡ God has bigger DREAMS!

Chapter 5

Chapter 5

GOD HAS BIGGER DREAMS!

THE FULLNESS OF THE HOLY SPIRIT ignited areas of my life that I did not know I had before. The passion and surrender in our communion grew deeper each day as I experienced a renewal of my mind (Romans 12:2).

To this day, I believe that encounter completely changed my mourning into dancing (Psalms 30:11), and took my worship moments to a new level, because I sang with a full understanding of what the Holy Spirit is and represents.

However, when I received Him, my spiritual lessons were far from over - in fact, they do not conclude for as long as God keeps us in this world. There was something big that the Lord wanted to trust me with, but before He did, I had to go through certain circumstances that would give me the maturity to receive it.

Before a great ministry receives great blessings from the Lord, it will go through teaching paths where it will gain the maturity it needs to grow within the waiting and the faith.

You may know me by the ministry God called me to be in, but I would like to tell you how everything began and how the Lord worked in me long before I became a part of the Barak group.

THERE IS PURPOSE IN THE PROCESS

The Word directly encourages us in 3 John 1, verse 2: "Dear friend, I pray that you may enjoy good health and that all may go well with you, even as your soul is getting along well" (NIV).

God's desire is to prosper us, not only financially, in all areas. But for that to happen - and as we walk towards the final purpose - we first need to go through a process, for it is necessary to verify whether we have the spiritual wholeness to steward what has been placed in our hands. This is exactly what happened to one of my favorite characters in Scripture: Joseph (Genesis 37).

God gave Joseph great dreams, but before he could see them fulfilled, he went through difficult times. The purpose was to reveal the reality and the plan that the Lord had already prepared for his life. However, despite what it had been revealed to him, Joseph had to experience situations where the reality was nothing like God's promise, which may have caused his big dreams to suddenly shrink, according to what his natural eyes were seeing.

Imagine Joseph, with his frustrated dreams, crying in helplessness, without understanding the reason why he was going through such difficult times.

Have you ever felt you were sinking to the point where the fulfillment of your dreams seemed unreachable? If the answer is yes, you may understand some of Joseph's mixed feelings.

For years, this man of God was constantly tested. He was thrown into a cistern; sold as a slave; forced to run for his life; imprisoned for the defamation of a crime he did not commit; despite being innocent, he underwent many tribulations. Joseph's character had to be strengthened, for he needed to be refined to become an instrument of blessing in the hands of the living God.

As the years passed, Joseph was able to understand God's plan through his trials. After everything his brothers had done to him, Joseph told them, "I am your brother Joseph, the one you sold into Egypt!" (Genesis 45:4). Joseph revealed his identity to his brothers after the Lord had greatly prospered him and explained them that the trials God had allowed him to go through had favored his maturity and character, placing him in a position of favor where he was able to work for the salvation of many different people. Just like him, we also need to understand the meaning and purpose of our upheavals.

Do you want to have God's support just like Joseph did? To walk from hard situations into a place of blessing and recognition? It is understandable, when we walk through the Lord's paths, we learn to ask for the best. But would you be willing to pay the price? That is another part of the story. It is no fun to be a slave and a convict. However, under those extremely difficult situations, the Father always has a purpose.

Dreaming of growing, expanding, and maturing is a genuine aspiration that the Lord supports - and even encourages. "Be strong and courageous, because you will lead these people to inherit the land, I swore to their ancestors to give them" (Joshua 1:6 NIV)

To dream is a good thing, but it always carried a counterpart: the works. The Scriptures state that "faith by itself, if it is not accompanied by action, is dead" (James 2:14). God wants us to be brave and diligent enough to go after our dreams in any area of our lives - at a personal or spiritual level, in our family, economy, ministry, etc. He intends to help us with this and increase our dreams to passionately fulfill His will, which is always perfect.

I am very much identified with Joseph's process, because just like him, I had to go through many challenges, although in different ways. Every beginning is hard, especially for those who serve on the Christian music area. You invest great amounts of time composing, recording, and rehearsing, and during the first months or years this is not always remunerated according to the basic needs of a person.

A DIFFICULT DECISION

After almost six years of dating and having gotten a new job after the one where I transcribed documents, I got married to the most intelligent and sweet girl I have ever met. Ana, a woman of God, patient, and someone that the Lord has used to promote me to where I am today. It has always been my dream to give her everything that a queen deserves, because she is, my queen.

Everything was going great in our early days as a family. It was all happiness. Financially, we were doing well, and I earned enough to support our household. After a year of being married, our love expanded with the birth of our daughter Amy, and without any doubt, having them both was a dream come true.

Despite this, three months after the baby was born, certain situations began to take place which put me in a position like Joseph. These circumstances made me feel as if I was trapped in a deep whole. I lost my job and my wife's green card had just been approved. In a very short period, everything got complicated.

We attended the appointment at the U.S Embassy to complete all of Ana's and Amy's documents. But to our surprise, our baby's papers were denied to travel with her mother. Just imagine our faces when we received the news. We cried bitterly, because the logical thing was that the documents of the baby would be approved together with the documents of her mother. It felt like our dreams were falling apart in uncertainty. What is more, our financial needs grew with every passing day, despite my tireless search for a job.

We asked for advice because we had to make an extremely difficult and rushed decision. My challenge was to convince my wife to put all her trust in me and leave the child under my care, to which she bluntly refused. Ana did not want to travel to the States and leave me alone. She was trying to convince me saying that we had opportunities to grow in the Dominican Republic, but to be honest, I considered it more convenient for her to finish her residence process in the United States, since we had been trying very hard to reach financial stability without success. It seemed like all the doors were closed and we could not see the exit.

Looking for a last alternative, my wife Ana and I went to hand out résumés. We were desperately asking the Lord to do something. However, no one ever called us.

After praying, we felt peace in our hearts, we desisted, and as a couple we agreed on a plan that consisted of Ana travelling to the States and applying for my residence once she was already living in that country. With our hearts torn apart we decided to go for what seemed better for our future. In the end, this was the only door that remained open, so we decided to hold on to God's will.

Crying at the airport, with pain in her heart and hopes of a better future for the whole family ahead, my wife walked through the threshold to the terminal she had been assigned. We said, with mixed feelings: "God is in control of our family and we won't be put to shame".

Our three-month-old baby and I stayed in the Dominican Republic. I took charge of the situation with great fear and uncertainty. I did not feel ready to be left alone and take care of my daughter. I was not ready at all! I was afraid she might lack food or get sick, but my greatest fear was not being a good father.

While watching the love of my life walk away at the airport, I repeated to myself several times with tears in my eyes that this was just a temporary separation, trying to find relief in that thought. However, I struggled with the pain of imagining that Amy could suffer like I did, by going through the same situation I experienced in my childhood when I was distanced from my mother.

I was shattered, I felt helpless. I wanted to be strong, but it was impossible for me. I wondered: Lord, will you really allow the permanent split up of my family? And I got a response, a gentle breeze that whispered in my ear, "Just wait on me". His answer was a promise to hold on to, so I courageously faced my situation.

Oh, how hard the days were despite my firm position! They seemed endless! While I got used to my new "normal", three years went by raising my little girl and handling her questions about why her "mommy wasn't there". As well as repeatedly explaining to my loved ones the reason why my wife was not present to raise her daughter. As if that was not enough, my heart was not in the best position and I was living as a single dad, but I had to defend my wife's honor in front of those who wanted to make me feel miserable and lonely.

Without making room for criticism, the three of us with God knew the sacrifice we made by preserving our home despite the distance. Not a day went by without Ana reaching out to me on the phone to find out about our daughter.

I was not able to understand then what God wanted to teach us with the whole situation. My wife sent us remittances every week, and I tried to administrate that money in the best way, but everything was spent on our daughter's needs. I spent months without buying clothes for myself. I even reached to the point of wearing out my shoes and dress in the same pants and shirt for a long time to go to church on Sundays.

In my room, while taking care of our daughter, amid our worst economic crisis, I sang praises, worshiped God, and declared that better times were coming.

Several people looked at me as a slacker and said I was not trying hard enough to find a job. I could imagine this came because of the cultural image that a stay-at-home dad has, but actually very few people valued everything I did, like giving everything of me and taking my role as a full-time mom and dad.

I can now understand that God was dealing with my character through my daughter. I was used to doing things fast and I had no patience, but I had to learn to be patient and calm, and gradually learn to comb her hair and change her diapers and her clothes.

With my baby girl in my arms along with a diaper bag, I weekly attended my church, Tabernacle of Worship, with fervent devotion to seek God's face - something that favored me before the Lord and gave my life grace, even in my darkest hours.

MY DREAM WAS BEGINNING TO COME TRUE

There, I met my friends from Barak, and I still remember it as if it were yesterday. They already had a group, with another lead vocalist. Before we became friends, our first contact was as members of the worship ministry in church. Angelo Frilop was the codirector of the worship ministry along with David Nolasco and Janiel Ponciano, the bass player. As leaders, they made me feel at home when I was in church, and the choir became part of my family.

Angelo and I became close friends. When he noticed my talent for singing, he offered me a job in his recording studio, as vocal director. My answer was automatic: "Absolutely, yes!".

When I arrived at his studio, I was impressed to see all the equipment that I had always dreamed of having. After being so immersed in the severe crisis that surrounded me, amid so much darkness, I could finally see a light for my artistic life.

If you move according to His purpose, our Father will put the right people in your way to help you get through the process. Just like Joseph had a friend in prison who recommended him to Pharaoh and was God's instrument to get out of the pit, Angelo was the channel of blessing God used to help me get out of such a difficult process.

You might be at the bottom of the pit, unemployed, and you might not see the exit, but you still need to keep moving in faith. I had been directing vocals for months, but I understood that I could not remain static. My duty was to keep working hard and be brave to move forward.

So, one day I armed myself with courage and went to the studio. I took advantage of what was supposed to be an ordinary day to break the silence. I asked Angelo how much it would cost me to record a demo. I knew that God could do something great with me, but I was not willing to wait for things to just happen out of nowhere, so I acted in faith causing them to happen. I could have stayed silent and kept working, but I learned that sometimes we need to move out of our comfort zone to cause God to start His work in our lives.

Surprised, Angelo asked me how I was going to be able to afford it (for he was aware of my situation). I told him that I did not have enough money to pay him at that time, but, even if I had to collect money from my whole family, I would find the way to do it. He trusted me and said, "Well, let's record that song!".

I had already written a song called "I'm confident", and I remember singing it many times with the guitar in front of my window. This song motivated me to be strong and wait on God, and even if I did not know when or how, His promises would be fulfilled in my life.

After recording the song, I got a call from Angelo, who was abroad at the time, and told me that while listening to my song God put in his heart a desire to record a complete album. He returned some weeks later and, together with his wife Raquel, they made me a proposal to begin with the recording of the album.

In my immense gratitude, I felt the confirmation that God was beginning to open doors for me. We worked hard for several months, and I could tangibly feel the Presence of God in each song, such as: «*Ven Espíritu Santo*» [Come Holy Spirit] and «*Todo va a estar bien*» [Everything will be fine], which were ready to be included in what was going to be my first album «*Nunca como ayer*» [Never like yesterday], by Robert Green.

After a long time recording it, and with only some finishing touches left (mix and master), for no apparent reason we found out there was a delay. God again seemed to be making a move and what should have been accomplished in a couple of days ended up taking several months. Despite putting all my effort and constant endurance to finish the project, God seemed to have other plans.

While waiting for the completion of my album, the Barak Ministry found itself without a lead singer. So, God placed in Angelo's heart a desire to invite me to be a part of the band. My immediate response was 'No', for we were about to finish the project we had already started, but he advised me not to make any rushed decision without praying and asking God first.

I left with a lot to think about, and I did not completely refuse his proposal. The truth is my dream was to be a solo artist, and it had always been like that. I sought advice and guidance with my mom, and she told me that what she had always wanted for my life was to see me releasing an album as Robert Green. Then, I asked my wife, and she did not see which would be the benefit of joining a band, and said she preferred for me to continue my vision as a solo artist. They certainly wanted to protect me from any disappointment, but I still had to decide, even though I was weighing against choosing Barak's offer.

Despite the many reasons for choosing to continue with my personal project, there was unrest in my heart. I knew I had to ask God before giving Angelo my final answer. For this reason, I sought His face in prayer, and I even prayed with my wife over the phone looking for that answer.

And amid those prayers, God confirmed it. His ways were designed for me to join Barak's ministry and His Spirit was confirming that it was not me, or the band, it was He who had a dream to fulfill, making us see that we did not have to pursue earthy titles, but the desire of His heart. In the end, He had promised to bless us and would do so in whatever position we were in. I did not understand at all what was happening, but I chose to obey.

When I made this decision, things changed radically, and God played His cards to show His favor over my family. My daughter, Amy, got her visa to get reunited with her mommy, and even though it was very painful for me to say goodbye after three years of my daily life as a father, I understood that it was necessary for God to do it, for He already knew everything that was coming for me as a part of the Barak band in the days ahead.

Sometimes it seems as if the Lord destroys the dreams, He Himself has built, but He is an expert in building the dreams that bless you and me the most, no matter what our aspirations may be. He says it clearly: "For I know the plans I have for you," declares the Lord, "plans to prosper you and not to harm you, plans to give you hope and a future" (Jeremiah 29:11 NIV).

> "GOD IS AN EXPERT IN BUILDING THE DREAMS THAT BLESS YOU THE MOST, NO MATTER WHAT YOUR ASPIRATIONS MAY BE."

BARAK

After making the decision to belong to Barak's ministry, God Himself began opening all the doors for me. Our songs found grace in radio stations and churches, and our music spread in a supernatural way all over the world. We received hundreds of testimonies of what the Lord was doing through our music.

The radical change in my story had me seeing myself again as a Joseph, but now from the perspective of someone who was being blessed, just like the man who found grace before the king and got quickly appointed to high office. I was able to see how God, with His abundant blessings, entrusted me with a very important place within His kingdom, so that I could reflect Him to the whole world.

We began travelling the Dominican Republic and the recognition of what we were doing voluntarily came along with hundreds of invitations to other countries. Consequently, after so many trips to the U.S. Consulate in Santo Domingo where I was always rejected, God granted me my first working visa to go on tour to that country. My first international trip. How amazing what the Lord was doing!

I felt an unsurpassable peace. Trusting God was my delight. The same God who had promised me that if I could truly trust Him, He would bless me. I went through many years of waiting, disappointments, rejections, and even on several occasions I doubted that this could actually happen, but our Father never forgets what He has promised: "I waited patiently for the Lord; he turned to me and heard my cry. He lifted me out of the slimy pit, out of the mud and mire; he set my feet on a rock and gave me a firm place to stand. He put a new song in my mouth, a hymn of praise to our God. Many will see and fear the Lord and put their trust in him" (Psalm 40:1-3 NIV). Even now, as I write these lines, it seems unreal to me to see the road full of ups and downs that I had to walk through to finally experience firsthand everything that for so long I had only imagined in my mind.

I left my country for the first time. I travelled to the United States to see one of my most awaited, prayed, and desired promises fulfilled: To be reunited with my family after four years of anguish and tears for not being able to be together. A year after my daughter left to be with my wife, I was not only able to be reunited with them again, but through every blessing that the Lord kept adding to my life, our family continued to grow, for God gifted us two more kids, Jayden, and Dyan, who brought even more joy before moving together to the same house for the first time ever in the Dominican Republic.

If we work hard to do things for the benefit of our own desires, leaving God aside, the doors that He wants to open will remain closed. We can turn the key, push the door, try to break the lock and nothing will happen, but if the Lord gives the order, the door will open. I have experienced it.

Our limited mind might never be able to imagine the gigantic magnitude of the Father's best plan for us. If my little dreams - compared to those of God - had motivated me to go after them, I might not have received everything that He gave me due to my obedience. I am not boasting in my achievements, but in His divine intervention every time that He came to me in my waiting with His gentle breeze, saying: "Just wait on me".

I know God has not finished with me yet, that His process continues in my life, as well as His plans for my future. I learned to walk in His footsteps, which will guide me to where He decides in the way that He wants.

I also learned to find guidance in His will, and not mine. If there is something I would like you to remember in the next ten or twenty years is the following: God has bigger dreams than ours!

He is an expert in rebuilding when we are torn apart; like a good potter, He shapes us to be a vessel where His glory will be poured out and takes us to places, we never thought we could go.

Sometimes God asks huge sacrifices from us, just like He did with Abraham; to leave his country and his people, and sacrifice his son, Isaac. Like Abraham, I had to make sacrifices for I did not want my family to be divided, and I also did not want to give up my solo career, but sometimes we must make personal abandonments to show God with our attitude that we are walking under His will and not ours.

The Bible has records of men who abandoned the divine promise for human promises and did not end well. We can also read about people who - despite what humans said - believed in the promise and reached God's glory. Let us hold on to God's promise, it will certainly come.

Looking back today, I realize I was in a process. I can now talk about it and understand it. God used the most difficult moments of my life to teach me how to depend on Him. That sacrifice is what makes us thank God every time, in any circumstance. Those moments of solitude, where I was unemployed and my family was not with me, helped me get closer to God and wait on Him. I learned that His thoughts are not my thoughts and that His timing is different to mine. "For my thoughts are not your thoughts, neither are your ways my ways," declares the Lord. As the heavens are higher than the earth, so are my ways higher than your ways and my thoughts than your thoughts" (Isaiah 55:8-9 NIV).

God's mind is unrivalled. If we were responsible of deciding what happens to us, we would always choose whatever is easy, fast, what we like and what does not hurt us, but God does not work in the same way we do - He is Supreme and Sovereign. When His will intervenes in our life it is always for our good, even if we do not understand it.

There will always be a roof we place above our dreams: our disbelief from thinking that we are not capable. However, He saw us before the creation of the world and knows us even better than we know ourselves. He knows the potential there is in every heart to carry out His dreams, which are immensely superior to ours.

The process has a purpose: To make us absolute dependents on God's will.

Even if you are amid a process, give thanks, because after going through difficult circumstances, you will be able to see the fulfillment of the great dream that God showed you, just like Joseph did.

Wow! You already know a lot about me at this point in the book. I laid my heart bare so that my testimony could be an inspiration to you, and you dare to give our Creator - the One who watched you since you were in your mother's womb - the opportunity to fulfill the plans He specifically designed for you.

Lets reflect together

Personally, evaluate the following questions and rate them from 1 to 10 (consider 10 as the highest score) considering how closely linked your dreams are to God's. Be honest!

1— Has God asked you for something really costly?

2— How willing would you be to give up a personal dream to fulfill God's dream for you?

3— Would you be willing to put your dreams in God's hands, even if His plan is very different from what you have dreamed of?

God wants to encourage you and challenge you to grow, but we need His guidance. Because His dreams are even bigger than yours, He will take you through the right paths, even if at first it seems that God made a mistake or was distracted. The process towards purpose is not easy, but it is amazing when you walk hand in hand with God. Evaluate your score: if it is a high score, you are right on track; if it is a low score, I invite you to take on the challenge and have the courage to sacrifice what you love to fulfill God's dream. Do this and be expectant to see a great future ahead of you!

Memoirs

childhood was full of a lot of love.
the first born in my home, as
as the first grandson of the family
th side. There were twelve brothers
my father and ten brothers from my
I remember how my whole family
me the love I needed to overcome
and take my first steps in life.

My childhood was full of a lot of love. I was the first-born in my home, as well as the first grandson of the family on both sides, there were twelve brothers from my father and ten brothers from my mother. I remember how my whole family gave me the love I needed to overcome my fears and take my first steps in life.

This is me riding a B.H Gacela exercise bike from 1980, demonstrating that I was ready to start a thousand adventures and feats in my life.

My sisters Catherin, Caroline, and I have always been very close. With them, I shared my first tears and joys, as well as the small fights between siblings that were not lacking in our daily lives. Together we learned to be humble, to forgive each other, and with a lot of love give each other a hug when it was necessary.

My mother María Brito worked for more than twenty years as a teacher in the city of Santo Domingo. A woman devoted to her family, a fighter, who loves to teach and help others at all times. In this photograph, she is in her armchair after taking a photo of my sisters and me. This image of her is one of the few photographs I could find of her because she is the kind of mother who prefers to sacrifice herself and always be behind the lens, capturing all the important moments of my childhood. Without her, my childhood memories would seem like just my imagination.

Before becoming a pastor, my father, Ramón Green, worked full time for more than twelve years as an inspector for the "National Lottery" in the Dominican Republic. Although he was exhausted most of the time, as he often walked home from work, he always had time to play with me and play his role as "Super Dad."

This is my entire family, my greatest gift from God. The cradle where all my dreams were born and the place where I learned to love God with all my heart. Thus, we will forever be united with God, because this is the true design of heaven for us.

Ana and I met while we were very young. She had something special that not only conquered my heart but also made my whole family fall in love! In our courtship, we realized that we were made for each other, and although we both had a lot to learn about a relationship and love, we held each other tight, ready to face and overcome the obstacles that awaited us in life.

Our wedding on September 13, 2008, was one of the happiest days of my life. Ana squeezed my hands very tight and overwhelmed with tears in our eyes, promised to love each other until death do us part in front of all our loved ones.

A year after we were married, our love extended with the birth of our daughter Amy. Without a doubt, having both of them was a dream come true.

I still remember this image of me praying with Amy after I left my wife Ana at the airport, who was on her way to the United States, due to the economic situation we were suddenly facing. At that time, I felt very sad and prayed to God to help me with this new and challenging task. I couldn't help but worry about how that experience could affect our daughter. I was afraid that she would lack food or get sick, but my biggest fear was not being a good father.

Our three-month-old baby girl and I stayed in the Dominican Republic accompanied by the great help of my mother, who not only helped me when I got home, but together we took responsibility for that situation. I did not feel prepared to be alone and take care of my daughter, but without a doubt, God helped me!

Several people viewed me as a lazy person and told me that I was making no effort to work. I suppose this was the result of the cultural image that men have in the household. Few appreciated what I was doing, although I was giving it my all and occupying my role as a full-time father and mother.

With my baby girl in my arms and her diaper bag, every week, I went with fervent devotion seeking the face of God at my church, Tabernaculo de Adoracion (Tabernacle of Worship). Before leaving to worship God, I made sure that I had given Amy her milk and checked her diaper.

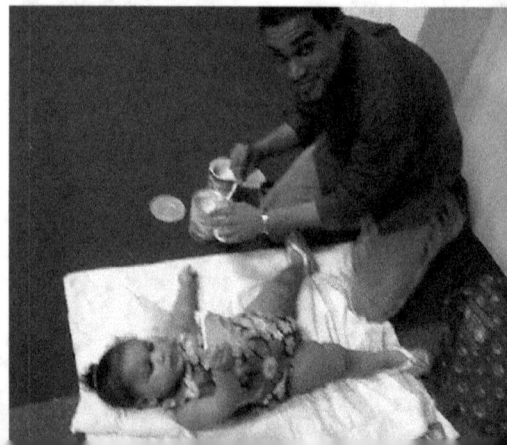

Jayden was born three years after Amy, in the United States, bringing even more happiness to our family and completing our dream pair. God rewarded me by giving me, my first boy. Despite our long-distance relationship, Ana traveled once a year to the Dominican Republic during her vacation time at work. This helped the family continue to grow.

Amy was very happy with her new baby brother, and Jayden enjoyed being in her arms. They have always been very close and prayed for a new brother. Amy wanted a sister and Jayden a brother. Three years later, God sent Dylan to us, and in the photograph to the right, we see how happy we are with Jayden because Dylan had come to complete the Green Polanco family.

A JOURNEY THROUGH DREAMS AND REALITY

"For I know the plans I have for you," declares the Lord, "plans to prosper you and not to harm you, plans to give you hope and a future."

Jeremiah 29:11 | NVI

I met my friends Angelo Frilop and Janiel Ponciano at the church Tabernáculo de Adoración (Tabernacle of Worship church). Before we became such Good friends, our first bond was as members of the worship ministry. Since the first day I met them, I knew that God was giving me something special, bigger than a song, even more powerful than a ministry, He was joining me with the brothers I never had and gifted me a family. The Lord began to move in a poweful way during our worship time and new songs began to flow. Here we are in a songwriting and recording session for Barak with our first album called "Thirsty Generation" on April 27, 2013.

This is our "Tabernacle of Worship" Church in the Dominican Republic, where God started it all. Almost all the songs of the ministry were born here, where months after entering the studio and composing, we recorded our first LIVE DVD "Thirsty Generation." Where we had as a guest our great friend Pastor Marcos Yaroide, who was the great surprise of the night.

God gave me the best spiritual father that any child has ever dreamed of having. Meeting my pastor Santiago Ponciano not only helped me grow spiritually, but, like a good father to this day, he has watched over my family and me, giving us the support and love we need.

After we made our first album, God began to inexplicably open doors. We met our manager Ismael Dávila and his wife Paola Díaz. They were the perfect complement to the ministry. Our first trip was on July 20, 2014, to Kansas City, United States. Then we visited Costa Rica and Puerto Rico. Months later we had the opportunity to travel for the first time with the whole family, on October 25, 2014, to Florida. Their names are (from left to right): David Nolasco, my family, Janiel, Milcy, Angelo, and his wife Raquel Reyes, Paola, Ismael and Josué Capellán.

MegaFest, Costa Rica. September 7, 2014.

Coliseo Bayamon, Puerto Rico, with Jesus Culture.

The concert, Generación Sedienta (A Thirsty Generation), with more than 8000 people.

During the first years of our ministry, we traveled to over 100 countries. God began to move in our worship in a supernatural way and we witnessed hundreds of miracles.

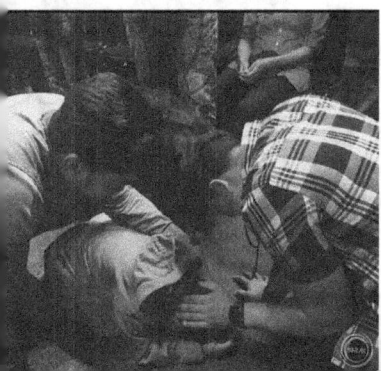

On April 5, 2014, I met Alex Campos, and he invited me to sing the song "He stole my heart," at a massive concert that he had in San Pedro, Dominican Republic. Months later we were able to record a song together for their new album «Waste of love», called «If I am with you», which encouraged us to continue opening doors in the Latin American market.

At the end of 2014, beginning of 2015, the Christian and secular media began to show interest in our music, and press conferences and interviews became part of our daily agenda in different countries.

On April 6, 2015, we were recognized as the highest representation of Christian music in our country, one of the most important awards at a secular level: "Premios Soberano".

On April 28, 2015, Los Premios Galardon (the Galardón awards), being the highest representation of Christian music in the Dominican Republic, awarded us as Group of the year, Outstanding Group abroad and also we won the "Gran Galardon" award (The Great Galardon Award) being the highest award of the night.

On January 25, 2016, God allows us to record our second musical álbum "Generación Radical" (Radical Generation), this time with the most influential singers of Christian music, such as Thalles Roberto, Redimi2, Christine D'Clario, Alex Campos, and Juan Carlos (Tercer Cielo). This day marked a before and after for our ministry. We worshipped God along with more than thirty thousand people in two sessions in the Dominican Republic.

This new album exceeded our expectations as it was nominated for the «Latin Grammys 2016». Our schedule had doubled compared to previous years so we had to adapt to a new lifestyle. Eat, work, talk with family and sleep in airports.

We wanted this Radical Tour to reach thousands of people and transform lives. One of the greatest victories that God gave us was to fill with more than thirteen thousand people the most important Coliseum of music in Latin America, El Choli Coliseo of Puerto Rico: José Miguel Agrelot. In our hands, we held a «Ticket of Recognition» for the record of sales in one week.

Being a minister of God brings both privileges and great challenges. I have missed being a part of many birthdays, college graduations, first days of school, marriage anniversaries, and other important days. Many hours I have spent talking on the phone with my family from hotels and airports. I have always tried to bring them to all my concerts to make the most of the time I spend with them. Being at home I usually play, travel, receive them when they return from school, visit grandparents, aunts and uncles. But, anyway, I can't deny that sometimes I cry when I'm traveling and one of my little ones says they miss me.

I thank God for all my ministry friends. Josué Capellán and his wife, David Nolasco, Agner Marte and his wife, Ismael Ovalle and his family, Ismael Dávila and Paola, Lucas Tazzo and family, Janiel, Angelo and Raquel who have become close family. Thank God that He has taught us to have a healthy separation between ministry and family. Whenever we can, we celebrate all birthdays and holidays together. Every day we come together and our family ties grow. In these photos taken on December 19, 2018, we are thanking God for the ministry.

For me, this hug meant a lot. It was one of those handshakes that are for life and that are full of sincerity, love, and a lot of tenderness, like that of this beautiful princess named Alondra, who told me when I was backstage, "I'm a fan of your music, and I want to tell you that I love you."

I will never forget the smile of Dariel, a 15-year-old young man fighting cancer, who ran to the vehicle that was taking us, hugged me, and with a smile on his face, said to me, "I love your songs, I sing them every day."

Every day I thank God for the legacy that I can leave my children. Gradually they have learned the importance of worship, and they say to me, "Daddy, we want to be like you. Take us to all your concerts as guests." My sweet Amy tells me: "I dance." Jayden says, "Daddy, I sing and play an instrument." And Dylan, the youngest, just says, "I'm going with you, daddy." It is beautiful to see them on stage and to know that even though their instruments are silent, their hearts are connected to heaven. I know that soon I will see them worshiping the Father and preaching the Word of God.

Recording of our third music album: Shekinah Live, with our friends Josh Morales (Miel San Marcos), Evan Craft, Redimi2, Kerroms Sims, Malachi Mendez. May 3, 2019

God has given the weight of his glory in our hands, and this is the most valuable thing we can have. Squeeze it so tight in your fist that it does not escape your side. Do not move if it does not move, and do not go if it does not go with you. His glory will be the one that puts grace in front of other people without forcing anything. That glory will represent us, qualify us and send us.

WISE DECISIONS
↗↗↗

Chapter 6

HAVING WISDOM IS NOT ABOUT MAKING THE DECISIONS WHICH IN OUR VIEW ARE THE MOST FAVORING, BUT *but deciding according to what God wants for us*

Chapter 6

WISE DECISIONS

Every one of us experience changes in life. Some change schools, jobs, or move houses. Others are constantly changing friendships, habits, clothes, among many other things. But changes are not always a bad thing. Sometimes they push us towards trying new things, different perhaps from what we were used to experience.

I felt confronted with that new lifestyle from the moment God changed the way I was living from a critical condition to a place of recognition. Despite how beautiful it is to receive the anointing and the blessings, you also expose yourself to being the target of difficulties, envies, temptations, and proposals, and I escaped none of these.

I know from personal experience that when walking towards what the Lord wants for you, you will find some dangers that can make you stumble - such as people's deceit, one's own pride and distancing from our God. I dare say that the enemy uses many people to present you with options that will ensure success without having to go through the process that the Lord has prepared for you to perfect you.

To be more specific: Some people will try to deceive you, taking advantage of your genuine aspiration to achieve a desire or a dream. In other cases, you could lie to yourself and believe that your success was gained on your own merits and not by the grace that the Lord has given you. Never allow your heart to become so arrogant as to believe you are the last bottle of water in the desert (to entertain this train of thoughts is very dangerous!).

I want to warn you that when you walk in the right direction towards the dreams God has for your life, you will get very tempting offers, of all kinds, but mainly in the financial area and as we know, the love of money is a root of all kinds of evil (1 Timothy 6:10). You and I must be careful with its nature, always searching the wisdom from above so that this does not lead us away from the purpose that the Lord has for our gifts and talents.

When facing these dangers, we, Christians have the great advantage of being able to seek God's face for our protection, just like we seek Him when we recognize Him as our Lord and Savior. The most important thing in the life of a Christian, is learning to have a close relationship with the Lord; to open our ears to hear His voice, which will always - in every situation - guide us towards the right choices.

Pretending to be a Christian on Sunday when we go to church is not that difficult. Externally, it will be enough to just raise your hands, sing praises and close your eyes during a prayer time. We prove we are true Christians when the problems of this world do not bend the ethics that we have learned from our Lord Jesus. That is, we act, decide, and operate wisely according to what was entrusted to us in His Word. If you choose to be obedient when going through the circumstances of this life, even if it costs you or harms you in the short term, then consider yourself to be a true disciple of Jesus.

If when facing a tough decision, for one reason or the other we walk away from the right path or choose to do the wrong thing, it could prolong the process to reach the plans that God has for us. I once heard: "The duration of your process will be determined by the decisions you made while you were in it".

I insist that to do this we must listen to God's voice (this is key), since having confidence in what He has said will stop us from making a mistake. If we listen to His voice, we can be confident in knowing that the decisions we are making have been previously approved in heaven and no decision aligned to the will of God could ever fail. We must trust Him when making our decisions.

However, it is not surprising but quite appalling, to see that many people quickly forget about Him and exclude Him from their own processes, and from this disobedience problems arise, because they did not take the time to listen carefully to God's voice.

We need to learn to place our decisions in God's hands, as well as to have self-control to act according to His principles and not on the whim of our emotions. For this, we need to acknowledge who God is, the value He has in our life and how important He is for us, because if we give Him the value He deserves in our lives, we will take Him into account when doing His will and not ours.

"IF YOUR DECISIONS AREN'T APPROVED BY GOD BEFORE YOU ACT, MAKE SURE YOU HAVE YOUR SEATBELT ON."

HOLDING ON TO GOD'S PLAN

I previously told you how I made the important decision of giving up my desire to be a soloist to hold on tightly to the hand of God, even if feeling helpless and powerless, believing I was taking steps adrift like Peter out of the boat.

In such difficult times, I walked by faith and - as I already told you - the only thing I saw was a record with my name on it. However, God did not share my enthusiasm. He was focused on putting to test the trust that I had placed in Him and in His plan, which, although it was not anything like mine, was much better.

Amid my process, I learned a great lesson: Don't try to do God's job. Let Him do it. The Word says: "Trust in the Lord with all your heart and lean not on your own understanding; In all your ways submit to him, and he will make your paths straight. (Proverbs 3:5-8 NIV)

What does this mean? God will constantly work to align you to the plan He has prepared for you. He knows what is best for you, what draws you away and near to His Presence. That is, if you dare to put your absolute trust in, He who knows everything about you, and let Him get involved in all your ways and choices, He will make your paths straight. In other words, we could say that He will shape the direction of your steps. And where is God planning to take you? Towards the perfect purpose He has prepared for you.

Many people make decisions lightly, without asking God about the desires of His heart. That happened to me for some time. I made the mistake of placing the foundation of my choices in the wrong places, such as: my talents, abilities, knowledge, and even my personality and influence. I was storing everything I had in torn sacks. I invested everything where my strengths led me and made me think it would be the best decision. However, I did not bother to ask God which was the plan He had designed for me.

Among those bad choices, I confess that I tried with all my strengths to record a music production, but I never managed to see any results. I also tried to be part of other people's musical projects and I only managed to wear my strength out without seeing fruits that brought me closer to God's purpose.

As you already know, I had to go through several processes until I became completely dependent on God. When formalizing my participation with the Barak Group, I found out that - just like me - the guys had experienced similar processes to mine before being part of the group. They told me that they had contacts available at radio stations and with important agents of the Christian environment, and even if they could help them to make their bands grow at an international level, their music never achieved the expected reach.

However, when we got together, we understood from our individual processes that perhaps there were certain areas that were not completely aligned to the true purpose, for we had clung to the idea that we could do it in our own strength, when we had evidently learned the lesson that we were not dependent on any of this.

> "YOU'LL KNOW HOW IMPORTANT GOD IS IN YOUR LIFE WHEN THE DECISION YOU MAKE IS IN HIS FAVOR AND NOT IN FAVOR OF YOUR OWN INTERESTS."

DOORS THAT NO ONE CAN CLOSE

Let me be clear: In the music field, sponsors play a crucial role to distribute music; labels are key to produce records; and contacts are relevant so that the albums are promoted and distributed effectively. I do not know in what or in whom you put your trust to propel whatever you do for a living, but there is a very thin line where we could be easily confused between these two things: to open the doors by our own means, or let God be the one who opens them. This I can assure you: It is better to wait for God's door to open, than to let our desperation forcibly open the wrong door.

Isaiah 22:22 says: "I will place on his shoulder the key to the house of David; what he opens no one can shut, and what he shuts no one can open" (NIV). The key of David is the representation of Jesus Christ and what He can do for us. It is not by accident that God said that this character was a "man according to His heart". He knew how to open the door that gave him access to a perfect communion with the Father. This is a very important text, because we sometimes trust our earthly keys so much (agents, radio stations, sponsors) that we do not comprehend those ministries are actually sponsored by God. Our one and only goal must be to acquire the key that opens His heart through our praise and surrender. He will be responsible for choosing which door to open so that the message received in intimacy can be spread for all to know Him. Those are doors nobody can close.

From that moment, we were amazed by every small but significant step we took in the Barak ministry; and even if there were many human attempts to make something great happen, it was not until we gave God freedom to do whatever He wanted, how He wanted and when He wanted to, that the doors of greatest blessing for the team began to open.

A beautiful anecdote took place in that decision of total dependence on God. We created two open tracks at the same time in the recording studio. In one of them, we recorded my voice, and at the same time we recorded the ambient sound in the other track, but there was no sound frequency that could be heard in it. We named the second track "Holy Spirit". And although there was not an actual sound, we understood that with that act of faith there was a channel available in the spiritual world that was being opened for the Holy Spirit to intervene whenever He wanted with his own Presence and melody. That is how we demonstrated our dependence on God. In this way, we asked Him to be present in every melody of our songs.

In the past, I wanted to sing with my own strengths, with my voice and my talent, but when I gave the Holy Spirit the place He deserved and allowed Him to sing, I became just an accompaniment.

From then on, we open a channel for Him, and I know that, even if no frequencies of recorded sounds are heard, He sings with us and joins us in worship. With this prophetic act, we brought a radical change in the way we did things, and we gave God permission to guide our projects with His beautiful and essential collaboration under the comfort of His times and decisions. We understood that no matter the audience measurements of any of our songs, He deserves the most important place in everything we do.

Since then, everything changed from one instant to the next. We had no need to force or insist on opening doors of promotion, because the One to whom we had opened the door and given freedom to move in our lives had the key and opened the doors of His will. Therefore, if we do not depend on God to make decisions and He's not in the first place, we will not move properly.

MISTAKES AND DISAPPOINTMENTS

We made some mistakes in the Barak ministry. For some time, we trusted people's work and not God. And when we rely in "professionals of the industry" we feel frustrated for placing our trust in a human being rather than in its Creator. When God does not feel involved in our decisions, He will close the doors and we will feel let down by people without understanding that it was God who allowed it so that we put all our trust in Him.

When our walk is guided by the Holy Spirit, anyone can feel the grace that is on your life, there is a sense of authority, even sponsors and labels can see there is something different in you, something that it is hard to find. That invisible peace that you transmit does not come from your talent, nor from your great or small fame, but from the grace that God poured on you since the moment you decided to become dependent on Him. This wise decision is the grace that will motivate those that can add something in favor of what you do, because they know that they are ultimately working for the Kingdom of God.

You do not always find people that value what God has given you, and in this part of the book I want to talk about those who have stood against you, who want to see you fall. Those who are filled with envy and want to be near you just to accuse you, and the enemy himself uses their lives to be a stumbling block.

The wisest advice I can give you to deal with them is to be joyful amid the false accusations against you. The Word of God says: "Blessed are you when people insult you, persecute you and falsely say all kinds of evil against you because of me. Rejoice and be glad, because great is your reward in heaven, for in the same way they persecuted the prophets who were before you (Matthew 5:11-12 NIV).

Personally, I take very seriously the part of "rejoice and be glad" whenever I hear rumors that are not true. I take the lyrics of a song by Juan Luis Guerra, based on Exodus 23:28 literally: "I will send hornets ahead of you to drive them out of your way". It also says in Deuteronomy 7:20: "Moreover, the Lord your God will send the hornet among them until even the survivors who hide from you have perished" (NIV).

The Lord is my defender; even if the accusers rise against me, He will send His angels to watch over me and protect me. When we are in God, we are safe, but if we walk without Him, we are helpless, prone to make mistakes, because there is no one to straighten our path. Glory to God for the absolute dependance on Him!

You will know you are in the peak of your relationship with God when He's the one who makes the decisions for you. You will realize there is a special treatment. So special that you will not want to do anything without feeling in your heart that He has previously approved it. By becoming dependent on God, you will also notice that He will daily put His trust in you, and with it, He will add virtues, gifts and qualities that will be eye-catching to others around you. The important thing is that you always let everyone know that the focus should not be in you, and that they are looking at the result of what happens when you are illuminated by the Light of the world: Jesus.

We need to remember daily that we are dust, brought to life by God's breath. Some people tend to define your worth by your achievements, without considering the One who really makes things happen. Others do not even see value in you. But when God's grace is poured over your life, people start valuing you only for what you have received.

There will be people who admire you and promise to bring solutions with selfish and greedy intentions. Probably most of them have never seen you, talked to you nor shook your hand before, but now they will want to get close to you. Wisely, I tell you, love them and ignore their works. They are like leeches that want to stick to you and benefit from your blessings by pretending to ingratiate themselves through compliments. If my ingenuity had made me fall into this poisonous trap, I would have been surrounded by people who only wanted to take advantage of my present state, and perhaps I would have based my identity on the praise that I received and not in what God said I was. This is so dangerous!

From the moment the Lord promoted me in my ministry, one of the toughest changes was that girls would write to me through social media with flirtatious innuendos, and I confess that, had God not been in my heart, I would have possibly made very bad decisions and would have been enslaved to my weaknesses. Diabolic attacks disguised as meek and beneficial opportunities began to multiply. Some Christian producers also got in touch with me, with all kinds of offers and even false promises of success on a secular level.

When we understand that God has a bigger plan with us, even if we fall, we will rise back up and abandon every plan that seems pleasant and that the enemy wants to present to us - whether with men, women, evil spirits, personal pleasures, or economic profit, because God continues to fulfill His purpose in our life. The enemy could come to offer us "pleasant" and momentary vanities even in the quietness of our intimacy. That is why I am telling you, be careful!

IN DANIEL'S SHOES

On many occasions I identified myself with the prophet Daniel, for example, when he was told to eat the King's food: "Daniel resolved not to defile himself with the royal food and wine" (Daniel 1:8 NIV). Everything comes from the willingness of the heart. If your heart is pure, you will know that, as appealing as a delicacy may seem, if its origin is evil, you must reject it. When we are guardians of the grace, we are offered so many things that we easily feel in Daniel's shoes.

Daniel was a wise young man pressured by a Babylonian system - the system of this world - which sought to change his heart to involve him in pagan acts that were contrary to his faith in God. Likewise, many young people are exposed to offers and pressures of this world that bring the opportunity to choose many things that seem good, but that end up promoting idolatry to oneself. This system offers us to delight ourselves with the delicacies of our "self-pride" and "ego", food that has not been appealing to me again since I met God, and just like the prophet, I had to say: "I won't defile myself with the food of the king of Babylon".

What was the king's food for me at that time? I could take advantage of my moment of fame to conquer girls and make many mistakes. However, everything else is now worthless if I never lose my dependence on the Holy Spirit. It is in Him that my true and only delight is found. There is no greater delicacy that could be compared to being faithful to my wife and to the purpose for which God called me.

The people of Israel walked around for 40 years until they reached their purpose. Sometimes we walk the same way. By making bad decisions we extend the process, spinning in circles to see the fulfillment of what God wants to give to us.

We are fragile and emotional human beings, and by experiencing so many changes, the mind and heart can get us in trouble. Jeremiah 17:9-10 says: "The heart is deceitful above all things and beyond cure. Who can understand it? I the Lord search the heart and examine the mind, to reward each person according to their conduct, according to what their deeds deserve" (NIV).

It could be easy for us to misinterpret what the impulses of our mind tell us. However, God is so good and merciful that advices us not to obey or let ourselves be carried away by the deceit of our own heart. But to bear good fruit with our works, that we may be approved before Him. Glory to God!

We not only hear the voice of our deceitful heart, but bad decisions can also be influenced by the voice of the enemy. When God places grace over our lives, the kingdom of darkness will automatically use every machination against you so that you stop obeying God's perfect will. Do not forget that when Jesus walked in the desert, He had a massive assignment. The enemy was aware of this, and his intention was to make Him fail. The devil knew the needs and fragilities Jesus had at that moment, so he offered Him food, riches, and even suggested He jumped off a cliff for the angels to catch Him.

Jesus, with a firm identity, knowing who He was, just used the written Word to deal with such attacks. What a great example He set for whenever we must make wise decisions! We must be focused and grounded in what God has written in His word about us, because we could make wrong choices. What the devil offered Jesus seemed tempting, because he was aware of the moment of bodily weakness He was in (after 40 days fast). He will do the same with you; he will use every situation where he knows that you could betray your convictions to tempt you. We need to learn not to make decisions based on the needs we are experiencing, but on the purpose, God has set for us.

It would not be crazy to think that Daniel abandoned his personal need and embraced God's plan, even if he really wanted to eat the king's food. When we attend to God's need, we are rewarded, honored with more grace. This accelerates the plan God has for us. When we overcome every personal test and temptation, God finds in us someone who has firm convictions in his identity as a son and entrusts us with bigger plans.

BEWARE WITH DELILAH

Another advice I would like to give you before we end this chapter is about friendships or family members that could be polluting your life. The influences around us not only come from the enemy, but from our close friends who could be used by the kingdom of darkness to guide us into making wrong decisions. Put your trust only in God and surround yourself exclusively with people that encourage you to grow, progress and who contribute to your faith. A toxic friendship could influence you to make very unpleasant decisions.

Samson is a good example of what we should not do. He let Delilah influence him. God had given him strength, grace, and a special gift, but this close relationship made him walk away from the purpose God had for his life and the consequence of this was his spiritual and physical death. If he had not let himself be influenced by Delilah, the story would have been different.

We must be very careful when choosing those who are around us because they have the potential to instruct us for blessing or for disobedience.

In my personal case I feel thankful and blessed to God for having put friends in my path who encourage me to daily seek more of God's presence.

The people you are surrounded by and that you choose to give your friendship to will not always be the most convenient to help you achieve your purpose. However, deciding who the right people are is not the result of how discerning or intelligent you are, but of laying down your will to the Father.

We all go through betrayals, disappointments and even sorrows for not always receiving in return everything that we give away. If your delicate heart has set its eyes on people and not on God, you could get to the point of giving up and walking away from the path that God has already chosen for you.

Proverbs 1:7 says that "The fear of the Lord is the beginning of knowledge", and that fear is not associated with being scared, but with the respect and reverence we feel when considering God as the primary figure in all that we do, before our own wisdom. That is, whenever I want to decide something by my impulses and knowledge, the fear of the Lord will force me to first think in what He would do, so that I am able to imitate His decisions, which will always be perfect.

A wise person is not the one with the greatest number of books read, knowledge and intelligence, but he who makes the right decisions; and what looks right to our eyes is not always what God considers to be the best. Let us learn from Jesus. When the Master was called to ministry, he decided to pick twelve people with plenty of flaws and imperfections. Jesus' choice was not due to lack of wisdom, but because He knew the Father's perfect will.

Being wise is not to make the decisions that appear to be the ones that favor us the most; it is to decide according to what God wants for us. No matter whether it brings suffering or not, the outcome will always be perfect, for His will is good, pleasing, and perfect.

You cannot learn how to act with wisdom in a course, at school or in college - it is something you acquire when going through different circumstances that force you to look yourself in God's mirror and imitate His decisions. God loves you and absolutely wants to expand and promote your ministry so that everyone who sees you can see the reflection of His grace in you. This anointing can only be obtained if we become dependent on what comes out of His mouth without obstructing with our own human hands the work of art that He's designing and building to show who He is.

Fear God, think what He would do before acting, and there will be no enemy, temptation, proposal, circumstance, envy or will of man that will be able to hinder the purpose for which you were called.

Let's reflect together

"The fear of the Lord is the beginning of wisdom; all who follow his precepts have good understanding", says the Bible. To make good decisions one must fear the Lord - and I have already explained the kind of fear I am talking about. Making good decisions is not the job of the isolated ones but of those who receive good advice and are surrounded by healthy friendships. That is why it is so necessary to evaluate who are we walking with on the path towards purpose.

1– How much do the people around you influence your decisions?

2– How much do you consider God when deciding?

I encourage you to go through your contacts and make the wise decision of walking away from those friendships that are not giving you good advice. You do not want to be like the people of Israel, that walked around for 40 years before reaching their purpose when they could have done it in four days. There's wisdom in God and involving Him in your decisions is the best thing you could do, for with Him you will never get it wrong.

Chapter 7

DEPOSITS IN GOD'S HEART

Chapter 7

DEPOSITS IN GOD'S HEART

IT WAS THE AFTERNOON OF DECEMBER 31ST, and I was doing some exercise, running as I usually do every week. But that day, as I was running one mile after the other, I felt in an overwhelming way the embrace of God full of grace. The shock led me to reflect on the year that was about to end; I thought about my life and how the Lord had guided my ministry.

As I meditated on this, I remembered how many times young people, journalists and radio and TV hosts ask me what they can do to reach significant levels of influence and fame. And to be honest, even if I wanted to give a simple answer, a recipe, or a formula that I could share so that everything goes the way they want, I do not actually have it.

However, after that experience while jogging, the Father placed in me the desire to write to you about what I do know and what I have acquired through the years in my ministerial journey. Those elements of ministry unknown to the public, but which gradually conquer the heart of God, are precisely the details that I would like to discuss with you. The Scripture teaches us in Matthew 25:23 that, if God sees that we were faithful with a few things, He will put us in charge of much more.

Have you ever wondered: Why doesn't God bless me? Why aren't the heavens opening in my favor, no matter how much effort I make?

At one point in my life this was my daily questioning. I believed that conquering God's heart was just a matter of singing, of doing things with the best intentions or praying and writing songs with heavenly synonyms such as "Holy, hallelujah, glory, etc."

And perhaps you, just like many other men and women, are waiting for an answer from God to achieve your dreams but have doubts about the purpose He has for you.

You might have seen a ministry grow "out of nowhere" - or at least that is your perception. Something that began small is now reaching more churches, more cities, and more countries than other ministries. But if you were close to that ministry, or investigated its beginning, you would find out that probably those results did not come "out of nowhere".

TREASURES IN GOD'S HEART

Constant sacrifice is the key. In the Apostle's Paul second letter to Timothy, he says: "That is why I am suffering as I am. Yet this is no cause for shame because I know whom I have believed and am convinced that he is able to guard what I have entrusted to him until that day. What you heard from me, keep as the pattern of sound teaching, with faith and love in Christ Jesus. Guard the good deposit that was entrusted to you—guard it with the help of the Holy Spirit who lives in us" (2 Timothy 1:12-14, NIV)

He also commands us in another text to pray continually (1 Thessalonians 5:17). By communicating with God, we recognize

His Lordship over us. When you pray, even if you feel nothing is happening in a specific moment, week, month, or year, you must know that with each prayer you are depositing treasures in the heart of God.

And what are these deposits about? Let me explain it to you this way. When you get paid a bonus or an extra salary, you go to the bank with part of that profit and make a deposit - this, if you are organized with your finances, which I highly recommend.

Why do we do this? To create a good credit history! Of course, you cannot create good credit overnight, but depositing our savings in a systematic way improve our financial behavior with the bank, and this makes your credit risk profile reliable. In simpler words, with this habit of saving, the bank says: "This person is reliable, we can give him a good credit limit!"

We could say that God works in a similar way with us. Sometimes we say: "Why should we consecrate ourselves to prayer?

Why does that brother or leader bend his knees with such devotion?" If you ask yourself those questions, you may not understand that those people are making deposits in God's heart.

We get pretty used to praying lightly, but we need to ask ourselves if that is the deposit we want to make in God's heart. We claim, "Well, I'm going to read a Bible verse and that's all, because I don't understand much of it". Please no! We must understand! That effort we put into knowing the Word adds up points in our Heavenly Father's bank.

> "TAKE YOUR REQUESTS TO GOD. HE WILL WATCH OVER YOUR INTERESTS AND MULTIPLY YOUR BLESSINGS."

There may be a Christian who seeks the face of God persistently, prays, serves and love others. Some time later, the gates of heaven open upon him and suddenly he becomes a minister with great global reach. But there may be another Christian that, even though he attends church, he sees no fruit due to his criticism, mockeries, and spiritual laziness.

If we metaphorically use the example of money (although in this book we do not talk about finances), I could tell you that the first one deposited million in heaven, while the second man only deposited a few bucks. Then he wonders: "How come suddenly (because we always believe these things happen from one second to the next) this person receives such great blessings?"

My answer would be that the first man was interested in adding credits in heaven, and so the riches of the kingdom are at his disposal with no limits, because his flow of input in the presence of God was continuous.

HEAVENLY PIGGY BANKS

I remember when my dad woke my sisters and I up at 5:45 am to worship the Lord. Somehow, this difficult sacrifice was a deposit without even knowing it and it brought the consequences that I enjoy today. I confess that I would have preferred to stay in bed, resting and hugging my pillow, but my father/pastor was responsible for leaving us a legacy of love and spiritual strength. He taught us the value of offerings, of depositing the first hours of the day in the bank of the heart of God. I did not understand it at the time, but what a great seed was deposited in my life!

One method many parents use to teach their kids how to save is buying them piggy banks and making them set apart a certain amount of money from their allowance to store it in that porcelain piggy bank. The goal of this teaching is for kids to understand that saving is a habit that is not so much related to the amount of money that we have, but to the attitude of being responsible with our resources. This is like what my dad decided to do with us, with the huge purpose of teaching us to make deposits in the heart of God through prayer, worship, sacrifices and an intense study of the Bible.

At first, when I was a boy, I would drag my feet into the living room, with sleepy eyes, a somewhat "foggy mind" and lazy muscles. But with time, my mornings became cheerful; swift pace and a voice willing to worship the love of my life, Jesus Christ, who took my place at Calvary and endured the punishment I deserved. As I have already told you, that is where my artistic career was born. The activity by which you may know me began in a living room, every day at 5 in the morning, when I was just a little boy.

I would then take to church that fervent desire for worship. There I cleaned, prepared the platform, tuned the instruments, visited the sick, and walked great distances to get home from church, for on many occasions public transport was no longer available that late at night. In conclusion, I did whatever it was necessary to selflessly serve the congregation, with devotion and no complaints. These are the valuable deposits that God keeps in His heart. Nothing we do for God is in vain - He never forgets everything we do for Him.

Service was part of my calling, even as a boy. I was passionate about working for the Father. His love and encouragement gave me strength. The almighty God filled me with joy and made me feel alive every time I was helpful in the wonderful work of expanding the Gospel.

As time went by, already as a 12-year-old preteen, in a sense I would have wanted to go out and play more, be with my friends who lived near my house, spend more time watching TV, or go to the movies more often, among other activities that could be more entertaining than going to church. In certain occasions, my friends did not want to make me part of their plans because they knew that at any time my parents would call me to go to some church activity, and I would leave things halfway. My friends could have thought that my parents forced me to do those things, but no - my family was instructing me to serve and teaching me the real value of the sacrifice we made for God.

I consider the habit of making deposits in God's heart from my childhood to this day one of the best investments I have done in my life, and I am grateful for everything that I learned during my upbringing.

THE BANK IN HEAVEN

Now, as an adult, I have a better understanding of finances and its similarities with the Kingdom of God. With the great difference that one consists of money and the other one of planting, prayer, service, and the Lord's faithfulness that comes from love.

In the present time, we generally rely on banks. In my country alone, the Dominican Republic, the Superintendency of banks reported public deposits of US$40 billion in the socalled multiple banks at the end of 2018. Apparently, we do trust banks! So how much more should we trust God, who is the Lord of everything that exists on heaven and earth? He is the same God that loves us in an indescribable way!

Rest assured that our generous Heavenly Father is aware of everything that we ask or do for Him. The nature of His character is to be a rewarder, and He does not owe anyone anything. So, He advises us in His Word: "Do not store up for yourselves treasures on earth, where moths and vermin destroy, and where thieves break in and steal. But store up for yourselves treasures in heaven, where moths and vermin do not destroy, and where thieves do not break in and steal. For where your treasure is, there your heart will be also" (Matthew 6:19-21, NIV).

Treasure this in your heart: "The Lord always rewards, for He cannot act in any other way. Our God is the Lord of rewards". If this concept is a motivation to you, you will not do wrong or fail for trusting that hope.

The Bible shows us in many different passages that the Lord will pay each one according to his work. Therefore, it will never be in vain to pray or serve the living God.

Let us see what God tells us: "Ask and it will be given to you; seek and you will find; knock and the door will be opened to you. For everyone who asks receives; the one who seeks finds; and to the one who knocks, the door will be opened. Which of you, if your son asks for bread, will give him a stone? Or if he asks for a fish, will give him a snake? If you, then, though you are evil, know how to give good gifts to your children, how much more will your Father in heaven give good gifts to those who ask him! (Matthew 7:7-11, NIV).

By the way, crying out to Him makes the difference, because it moves the heart of our God. For a long time, I thought that I knew the Father's will, but then I walked away from a consecrated life, while trying my luck with my own strength.

Yes, it is true, "I can do all this through Him who gives me strength" (Philippians 4:13), but this statement also applies to the opposite case:

"We can do nothing without Christ" (John 15:5). That is why it is essential to know the will of the Lord we serve.

THE CREDIT OF GRACE

During that stage of my life in which I had decided to go after human credits to seek for the attention and applauses that my ego needed as if they were oxygen, I had to face difficult consequences for not seeking first the Kingdom of God and His righteousness (Matthew 6:33). I wanted to settle for the additions, which, ironically, I did not get either. When our heart diminishes the importance of getting beneficial things to focus only on worshipping, God's blessings come and the heavens open.

Our salvation is by grace but rest assured that he who deposits in the bank of God's heart more prayer time, love for His Word and serving time here on earth will receive greater attention from our Savior. "For we are God's handiwork, created in Christ Jesus to do good works, which God prepared in advance for us to do" (Ephesians 2:10, NIV).

When we understand that the Christian life can only be lived by grace, we become like the one who grabs a credit card and deliberately spends as if that money was his. If you know that you only live by grace, but you neglect your prayer time, reading the Bible and your spiritual life, you enter an "overdraft time", and you delay the purpose that God has for your life. When the crisis comes, you are not ready to face it with the characteristic peace of a son of

God. This simply happens because you have not made deposits in the bank of God's heart.

For a while I experienced what Matthew 15:8 says: Even though I sang praises in different churches, I was honoring God with my lips, but my heart was far from Him. Then the crisis came because things were not working as I had planned. In the face of difficulties, I gave up, and walked with a defeatist attitude for a season, since I forgot what I had learned at home: to make deposits in the heart of God.

How did I get out of my own desert? Crying out, declaring the sovereignty of our God, diving in His Word, making up for the lost time and making new deposits in His heart, locked in the solitude of my room.

The Father wants to be with you, speak to you, and reveal His plans for your life. That is why it is not enough to tell your acquaintances that you have faith; you must live it intensely, obeying the Word of God.

Perhaps you have asked yourself, "What are you saving for?" Personal financial specialists call savings an "emergency fund". The characteristic of these deposits is to help us face unexpected problems that demand an amount of money that has not been foreseen in our budget.

Although deposits in God's heart are not only useful for dealing with problems, having deposited prayer, service, fasting, and Bible study time empowers you to handle any kind of crisis you may face.

Likewise, we must seek to invest our time and energy for the benefit of the Kingdom before all the extra things that could come for our own good. Big deposits are made in God's heart when we understand that serving is a priority, just because we love His presence and value His grace.

In the same way that deposits in God's heart can help you achieve the purpose for your life, there is also the possibility of forgetting your Father and falling apart, no matter how great your success has been. Sometimes we do not feel God's support because we have stopped making deposits in His heart. However, we continue to work in ministry because we are committed to pleasing people rather than God.

If we cannot fool the banks, let alone God! Some ingenuous people deposit huge sums of money in the bank just days before asking for a loan. However, this will not guarantee they will be granted the loan they need, since the financial institution recognizes these tricks from miles away. How much more will the omniscient Father see our true intentions? Let us not try to win God's support with a one-day long prayer, believing it will be enough for an entire month. In the same way credit lines are built day by day before financial institutions, your relationship with Christ will be strengthened from the constant deposits made from true intimacy and prayer.

The Lord wants us to have a vision that empowers us to achieve goals that include spiritual growth and personal development, since we are more than conquerors through Him who loved us (Romans 8:37). And you know why? Because we were called according to His purpose.

By the end of those three long miles that I ran that last day of the year, I could not help but thank God for His goodness in revealing me this great teaching. Sunset fell, I had a shower, played with my kids, looked through Barak's activity planning and enjoyed the huge dinner my wife had prepared, without forgetting to welcome the new year by making deposits in God's heart.

> "VALUE YOUR TIME ALONE WITH GOD, BECAUSE EACH SECOND SPENT IN THE SECRET PLACE WILL GUIDE YOU TO THE INTIMATE VAULTS OF HIS HEART."

Let's reflect together

Keeping a constant communion with the Father through prayer is the fuel we count on to accompany us on the journey. Many fail to see the importance of prayer. Every time we pray to God, we are making advance deposits in Heaven's bank. And let me tell you: those who think prayer is boring have no idea that prayer is a dialogue and not a monologue. Prayer is a sweet conversation between a Father and a son.

I want you to become a great worshiper. No matter if you sing or not, we are all worshipers, and for that reason I would like you to answer the following questions:

1– Am I dedicating time to prayer throughout my day?

2– Do I pray enough to recognize my Father's voice when He speaks to me?

Recognizing the voice of your Heavenly Father is part of an exercise that should be practiced daily - only then you will be able to recognize it amid a great murmur of confusion. Make prayer a non-negotiable part of your daily life!

Chapter 8

THE CHALLENGE OF THE CRISIS

Chapter 8

THE CHALLENGE OF THE CRISIS

ON MY WAY TO THE AIRPORT, surrounded by suitcases and the logistics of the trip, I received news that struck my heart in a deep way. I confess that it did not completely break my spirit or made me lose my faith, but it did push me into a mental struggle. If it were not for the peace and confidence in the supernatural power of the Holy Spirit, I would have considered returning home and postponing the concerts we had set for that week.

However, I know well who do I trust and what is my calling, so these news didn't stop me from boarding my plane and taking advantage of that travel time to write this chapter and tell you the challenge that I've been through for a long time. This challenge has motivated me to be more dependent on God amid the crisis, and to grow my trust and faith in the God of miracles.

I wish our Father uses this story to minister peace to you, and to strengthen your life amid whatever challenge you might be facing. I am ok, God is with me, and He's with you too. So, let us dive right in!

You might think that at this point in my life and my career everything is perfect, and that my successes and achievements have freed me from difficult situations. However, that is not true. God tests us so we can examine our relationship with Him, as well as assess how much faith and obedience we have for the next plan God has for us.

I can assure you that when He wants to bless you and take you to a new level of surrender, service, trust and manifestation of His Spirit, He will allow for you to experience rough moments. Although they can cloud the scenery, they also refine our capacity to experience in our own flesh that famous phrase that we tend to hear daily: "It is not by sight but by faith".

That is what happened to me, but in the most unexpected way. My heart experienced uncertainty from a call in which they informed me that my mother needed surgery, again.

With this terrible, repeated - but necessary - feeling, I will describe to you the process by which, for many years, God has shaped and perfected my faith. Despite so many tears, complaints, and doubts, walking through His mysterious paths has made me embrace His Presence to keep me on my feet.

A CONFRONTING REALITY

It all begins with an excellent relationship between a mother and her son. Ever since I remember, I found refuge in my mother - a woman of faith and prayer, willing to sacrifice everything for the sake of her family. She is one of those mothers who you rarely see crying and who always has the right words.

One of the things I admire the most about her is that since I was a boy, I have always heard her declaring, praying, and establishing the Kingdom of God in our home. The hallways of our house were filled with words of blessing and exaltation to the name of Jesus; no matter how early in the morning it was, her prayers did not cease. She still carries this characteristic. I do not know if there are many mothers like her, and that is why I have always considered it a blessing to have her.

As I slept, she used to come into my room and declare blessings over my life, with phrases like: "Lord, I dedicate my son to You, just like Hannah did with Samuel. "My beloved Father, I place him before You, I leave his life in Your hands, protect him, bless him, guard him".

On several occasions I was able to overhear her prayer times and how moved she was by the Presence of God in her room. I was used to the sounds of her fervent passion and dedication that overflowed from her intimacy with the Father. However, there was a night that marked the history of my life and welcomed me into one of the most significant challenges I have ever faced.

Although I don't exactly remember the reason why I was walking through the hallways of the house that night, I perfectly remember the sound of a heartbreaking moan that caught my attention. With curiosity, I walked towards the place where this sound was coming from. I could not identify it as her usual time of intercession; this time I could perceive that she was in deep sadness.

Surprisingly, I ended up right in front of the door of my mother's bedroom, but because it was so late at night, I did not want to invade her space. Conflicted about not wanting to break into her privacy and wanting to know what was going on, I boldly allowed myself to knock on her door with a light and fearful knock and decided to wait for her prompt response.

I waited a few minutes, but nobody answered, so I insisted and knocked a few more times. As far as I could listen, it seemed as someone was moving fast inside the room, and in my uneasiness, I could not keep waiting, so I knocked harder and even tried to open the door, without success. After several minutes - at my insistence - she opened the door and asked me: "What is it?"

I immediately knew she took her time to open the door because she was trying to wipe her tears; she did not want me to see her like that. Yet, it was evident: her complexion was telling me that something was wrong.

Nervous and with trembling legs I said, "Mommy, you're crying. I heard you crying out loud in your room, what's going on?" It was very hard for me to look her in the eyes because I had never seen that kind of tears. I had never heard or seen my mom cry like that before. And although she tried to put her best face to speak to me, what I saw in that moment was no longer the cheerful look that I knew.

With her gaze fixed and a sea of thoughts, I waited for an answer. However, she just hugged me. Those seconds seemed like years to me. They were so tense that, just by looking at her, tears burst out of my eyes, even without knowing what was going on.

She suddenly broke the silence in the middle of that strong hug, and with a quavering voice said, "Son, I've always dreamed of seeing what God is going to do with your life; I've always dreamed of seeing your children grow up. My greatest desire has always been for God to give me health and enough years to be able to enjoy all the blessings for which I have prayed, and many of my desires are about being able to see the fulfillment of God's purpose in your life to the fullest".

So far everything seemed uncertain and quite touching, but her answer did not fully clarify the news I was waiting for her to give me. So, she then closed her tender, loving statement with a terrible phrase, "I was diagnosed with cancer".

Usually, the first reaction of someone who is faced with this kind of news is to burst into tears, yell, complain, and give place to the worst possible thought that tells us: death is around the corner!

However, when I heard this, I felt the Holy Spirit coming up to me and taking me back to a situation that had taken place many years before, where something similar had happened, but in that case my mother and I had opposite roles.

I was taken to my childhood, where I remembered a doctor giving me a negative diagnosis about my health. Although this happened several years ago, I can still remember that moment as if it were today, when she responded with an aggressive faith, cancelling the unfavorable diagnosis that the doctor was giving me.

She stood up filled with strength and said to him, "Well, look. What will be accomplished in the life of my son, Robert, is not even close to what you have just said about him! What will happen in his life is what God has established. He will be a prophet to the nations, light in the darkness, and a voice proclaiming there's salvation in God. My son is life and not death, so I do not accept your diagnosis!"

I remember those words came to my mind with that same intensity, and with the boldness of the Spirit I fixed my eyes on hers and repeated the same scene we had lived many years before, saying, "Mommy, what will be fulfilled in your life is not the word of a doctor but what the Lord has said, and He has declared life, light and blessing over you, not curse nor death".

Even though what was happening in my mother's body was a reality, it was not the absolute truth that we were believing for.

We resumed our hug and began crying, not out of fear, but because of the touching moment when we uttered the name of Jesus and a torrent of hope poured upon us. Although our souls were very sad, they had begun their training to a journey of many trials, emerging from the affirmation of what God had said and not what the doctors were declaring.

In the middle of the process, we learned to rest and increase our confidence in the God of miracles. To this day, she has undergone over twelve surgeries in the last sixteen years since she has struggled with this diagnosis, and we have seen God's hand intervene in every single one of them.

Amidst everything that God was doing with the ministry and the privilege of allowing me to go to the nations carrying His message, declaring healing, and seeing miracles happen, there was a miracle that had not yet taken place at home.

I have seen God work miracles through my worship, which has caused the move of His hand. And even though it was amazing to hear so many testimonies of people who had received their miraculous answer, I could not understand how much time I was supposed to wait for my own answer. I finally realized that God's will is sovereign, and He decides the precise time in which we will see His favor.

> " WHEN WE LEARN TO DEPEND ON GOD, WE DON'T EXPECT TO SEE OUR MIRACLE STRAIGHT AWAY, BUT WAIT PATIENTLY FOR THE RESPONSE OF HIS WILL."

THE STING OF THE PROCESS

No matter how much God uses you, that is no guarantee that He will have special treatment with you, nor will it make you untouchable or exclusive, but it will allow circumstances that bring out the best of you to take place, just like it happened with Paul the Apostle. I feel identified with the process where he described there was a situation that afflicted him. He compared it to a sting in his flesh, which was allowed in him so that he could learn to rejoice amid his anguish. He also says that even though he asked God to take it away from him, He did not (2 Corinthians 12:7-10).

This amazes me because, evidently, the Lord is showing us that these negative situations are necessary to refine us and become worthy inhabitants of His Kingdom. The Bible says in Acts 14:22: "Strengthening the disciples and encouraging them to remain true to the faith. «We must go through many hardships to enter the kingdom of God» they said". Although we don't know exactly what was afflicting Paul, his example shows that God allowed this situation to perfect something in him.

In my case, the sting that burdened me was the pain and the extensive illness of my mother. No matter the platforms, concerts or nations, God was personally dealing with my dependence, trust, and faith in the privacy of dressing rooms and hotels, where I felt exposed to the thought that at any moment, I would receive a tragic call.

When I received this word, I somehow managed to explain why God wanted to work in my heart - no matter everything He was allowing me to experience through my calling. At times like this, we are not able to see the "good" in a difficult situation, but God insistently repeats to us in His Word that it is all necessary. So, I want to give you different verses that have accompanied me in moments where I cannot comprehend the magnitude of my process and what I should do amid it.

"Dear brothers and sisters, when troubles of any kind come your way, consider it an opportunity for great joy. For you know that when your faith is tested, your endurance has a chance to grow. So let it grow, for when your endurance is fully developed, you will be perfect and complete, needing nothing" —James 1:2-4 (NLT).

"God blesses those who patiently endure testing and temptation. Afterward they will receive the crown of life that God has promised to those who love him" —James 1:12 (NLT).

"So be truly glad. There is wonderful joy ahead, even though you must endure many trials for a little while. These trials will show that your faith is genuine. It is being tested as fire tests and purifies gold—though your faith is far more precious than mere gold. So, when your faith remains strong through many trials, it will bring you much praise and glory and honor on the day when Jesus Christ is revealed to the whole world" (1 Peter 1:6-7 NLT).

Those who have gone through the experience of being close to people with this disease know the result of advanced cancer, which in my mother's case was Grade 4. However, by recognizing that God was working in me I began to rejoice in my process, because even if there was uncertainty about the end of this illness, God was being glorified, both in our integral growth, as in the miracle of seeing my mother wake up after each surgery.

To this day, God has strengthened us and allowed us to see His miracle every time that my mother wakes up. This fills us with gratitude for being able to see His hand and favor every morning.

There is a phrase we learned from Julio Melgar, a renowned worship leader who went through a similar process with cancer. And although he passed away still struggling with this disease, he left us a great lesson of gratitude by saying: "We ask for a miracle when the miracle actually happens every day."

Many people only see important ministries that travel to different nations serving the Lord and this makes them think that those who are part of these ministries are excluded from difficulties, processes, and hard circumstances, ignoring that this requires them to go through certain situations to keep standing with their calling.

Perhaps the crisis you are going through now has made you doubt, distrust, or even think that God has forgotten you. The truth is that desperation makes you magnify what you are living right now in a negative way through complaints, doubts and other pessimistic things. Inversely, this situation has come to produce something bigger in you, to believe that the best is yet to come, refining your ability to resist, knowing that everything that we experience is temporal and we are not meant for an unfavorable ending – in fact, we have a glorious destiny. "For our present troubles are small and won't last very long. Yet they produce for us a glory that vastly outweighs them and will last forever!" (2 Corinthians 4:17 NLT).

At a difficult time, David, the psalmist, wrote: "I waited patiently for the Lord to help me, and he turned to me and heard my cry" (Psalm 40:1 NLT). Many only expect from Him blessings and anything that publicly makes them look successful, completely ignoring the waiting time amid the trial that he allows us to go through to perfect us.

In the same way a muscle grows through a process of resistance when working out (something that could be painful), so does faith.

It gets perfected and increased through endurance, when we undergo different circumstances, where everything forces you to put your trust exclusively in God's promises. And just like your body needs more and more weight or pressure to keep growing, that is also the way God will help you get through the situations that are hard to cope with to increase your trust and rest in Him.

It is just like a videogame, where every new level you access gets a little more complicated, forcing you to find strategies, lives, and skills to get to the next one. That is how our Christian life is; the greater the magnitude of the place where God wants to take us, so will be the test that He will hand to you to get the best out of you.

Your relationship of trust with the Father must grow. If your dream is for God to trust you with great places to deliver His message, He will first have to make sure that you trusted Him blindly during your trials and processes.

This does not make God the bad guy, on the contrary, He tells us: "For I know the plans I have for you," declares the Lord, "plans to prosper you and not to harm you, plans to give you hope and a future" (Jeremiah 29:11 NIV).

Even when we go through situations so rough that do not seem like the plans God said in His Word He had for us, we cannot complain, let alone allow the enemy to point us out to make us feel guilty, creating the foolish belief that we must have done something wrong to deserve such a terrible present. With all authority and love I say to you: don't believe him! For neither you, nor even the enemy know the end of your situation. And if there is something that I can assure you with all my heart is this:

God is not a liar! And He will fulfill the plans for good that He has for your life.

Just as He allowed it in Joseph's life to prove how strong he could be, God will also do it with you. Every crisis will give you the chance to blindly believe and in your final state you will be able to give God the glory out of gratitude. For He was always able to see what you could not.

THERE'S A TEACHING IN THE PROCESS

In the moment of greatest anguish and distress for my mom's situation, I had to decide whether to cry, give up, curse God, complain about how unfair the situation was, or raise my hands and worship Him amid the process.

My circumstance did not prevent me from continuing going after my call. For months I continued travelling and singing in many concerts and in different countries with this uncertainty, but at the same time, with a silent and passionate moment of intimacy with the Lord that provoked me to cry out, saying: "I know that You're going to do a miracle, I know that You're faithful with my family and if You had the power to heal me years ago and I've received hundreds of testimonies of the miracles that You've worked through my worship, in this moment I believe that You'll heal my mother with that same power".

There have been many negative diagnoses given to my mother, but the only thing I have agreed with according to what the doctors said is that she is a walking miracle, because we are aware that we should have seen her go a long time ago, but it is beautiful to know that God has not decided to take her from this world yet. Through her we have continuously seen the manifestation of the supernatural power of God, and, thanks to this, more and more members of my family are believing that the God of miracles is real. Hallelujah!

I have never seen my mom falter, not even amid the many crises she has been through. Even in the worst moments, I have only seen a strong woman, filled with faith.

Even though the testimony starts from my mother's suffering, being her son did not exclude me from the whole crisis and mental struggle with fears that has not managed to bring me down in all these years. This prepared me to not give up and strengthened my faith to reject any prognosis about her death. Today, I can say that I have seen God's hand do the impossible before my eyes.

And every time I see her now, my heart no longer grieves but rejoices in what the Lord has begun and will finish at any moment. My mom has been teaching us all a great lesson: that even when going through the biggest crisis of her life, she is chosen to worship God with dance, joy, and words of praise, showing us what a true worshiper's heart really looks like.

If God completes the miracle, glory to Him! If not, He will still be glorified, because I recognize that dates and times belong to Him (see Acts 1:7). My heart will remain humble towards Him, willing to receive the good and what seems bad, so that He may be exalted.

«THE MOST IMPORTANT THING WHEN BEEN TESTED IS NOT TO COMPLETE THE PROCESS FAST, BUT TO DISCOVER WHAT GOD WANTS TO TEACH US AS SOON AS POSSIBLE.»

A FAITH LIKE ABRAHAM'S

My mother, María, will always represent a banner of faith in whom we can see an example of how not to compromise one's beliefs. No matter what we may be going through, she reminds me of hundreds of teachings and sermons that I have heard about Abraham's story, and they are all related to the processes he had to go through to end up becoming the "father of faith".

Although I always felt identified with God's intention to make this man a legacy of surrender and sacrifice with a huge descendance, it was not until I experienced it firsthand that I realized the magnitude and challenge of the crisis Abraham had to go through to become an admirable example within the Bible (after Jesus, who is the perfect example).

I learned that "Father of Faith" is not just any title, but that when we want to become great examples of faith and impact generations, certain situations will come to pass where the Lord will have to break and crack things to make them new and help you become a son of God, with the foundation of knowing in whom you have believed.

Abraham went through different challenges where he just obeyed, and I feel identified with them. Firstly, God asked him to leave his land and kinship - that is, his comfort zone (and he did so without hesitation). Then, He asked Abraham to kick his firstborn, Ismael, out of his house along with his mother. Lastly, He requested Isaac - the son of the promise, the one "whom he loved" - to be sacrificed on the altar. And for what we know, he was willing to do it.

Even if we cannot compare our faith with that of this man, we can understand that he had to go through different crisis, one harder that the other, and all of them seemed to have a deadly ending. There is a similarity with my story, and I dare to say that the great things that have been accomplished through my life and ministry come from the obedience and permanent trust in what God says, surrendering whatever He may ask from us. No matter how many more crisis I must face, even if death feels close, I know that, like Abraham, my worship and obedience will impact the future generations.

God will allow difficult situations in our lives so that we learn to understand that we do not depend on ourselves, but solely on His grace. Job could have cursed God but never did it, even though everything he had was taken away from him. Recognizing the unfathomable sovereignty of the Creator is also part of faithfully managing a life of blessing.

You who are now reading these pages may tell me, "Robert, you don't know what I'm going through". I certainly do not know what you are going through, but I can tell you what I have learned: If my mother has the ability to rise, you and I can equally rest in the Lord, no matter the slight and momentary tribulation we may be going through.

My mother is a warrior of the Lord. Strong as an oak tree, with an unshaken will, and always willing to trust God no matter the circumstances. Today, I have the opportunity of testifying what the Lord has done. Believe me, if you manage to find new strength by reading my story and you notice there is something that is making you believe in God more and more each day, this will be the best reward I could receive after having overcome each of our processes.

The battlefield for spiritual warfare is mainly in your mind; if you can win, you will experience the absolute peace and confidence in knowing that no matter what your eyes may see, God is with you, and He is in control over everything.

My mother has been an example for her three children, and I want to dedicate this chapter to her, as a symbol of honor and respect for who she is. There is no special way in which I can pay her back for everything that she has done for me, from the way she has raised me and set me apart with her prayers, to the long mornings where she allows me to be with her in her processes, to experience them closely. For all this I thank God.

Because of the example of my mother, the "victorious one", I can now walk amid a crisis with a strengthened faith. I will never stop talking about the God who has enabled me to understand through my mother the greatest lesson that I have received: The Father is with us amid the crisis.

Let us meditate together

How many times have we heard about the subject of faith, and we have even claimed to have it as part of our spiritual inventory! However, faith is a seed that needs soil to grow and develop, and it must first crack so that what's inside of it can grow. Times of crisis are like the soil, where one must plant faith for it to germinate and see the fruits. The Lord warned us that in this world we were going to have trouble but that we had to trust and have faith because He has overcome the world.

1– Are you going through a time of sickness, economic challenges, family issues?

2– Do you recognize that there is a seed of faith in your life?

What you are going through may not be easy, and I can understand that because - as you have read in this chapter - I had to walk through that valley of pain and I am still in it, but I want to encourage you to plant your seed of faith just like my mom did, and trust that God is in control of every single thing. And remember that God is also walking with you through the challenge of the crisis.

Chapter 9

Sleeping, singing and traveling

Chapter 9

SLEEPING, SINGING AND TRAVELING

FOR A LONG TIME, I was one of those who admired how renowned ministers traveled the world carrying their music or conferences. And as a young man, with a heart full of God's dreams, I cannot deny that I was captivated by how fun and interesting it looked to travel through many places doing what one loves.

Since I did not sing for the world but for God, I found that lifestyle attractive and at the same time I liked the idea of many noticing what I was able to do with my talent. As I grew up and matured, I realized that being a servant of God did not only come with the reward of getting to know other countries and people, but also with being given a certain time to be up on a stage, in a city, an event or in a conference. But that kind of service to God goes far beyond all these blessings.

I cannot deny that I admired the lifestyle more than the commitment that a minister must undertake. I was always focused on how fun it looked to sing in front of thousands of people from different parts of the world, be famous and admired by the audience. I found the way in which important ministers carried appealing God's Word.

Since I was born in a pastoral home, I had never seen the ministry in any other way, so my first motivations were based on wanting to show my singing skills. I had never taken the time to think about what a minister should do for God to take him to the nations. This is where I got stuck for a long time, because my aspirations were based on the benefits of serving God, but not on the commitment needed to receive that reward.

If you have not skipped the previous chapters, you have already read about some of the processes that I had to go through to make this "sleeping, singing and traveling" a reality in my life.

BACK STAGE

When I was way younger, I dreamed of this present from an immature position. This is currently happening to many young men and women motivated by what they see, unaware of the responsibilities, commitments and sacrifices found backstage. Yes, it looks fun, but I want to tell you that for this to happen we must be very prepared; otherwise, it will not be so "fun" anymore.

Sleeping, singing, and traveling is an attractive expression at first sight, but if we really want it, we must assume a great commitment with God, or else we would be putting a burden on our shoulders that will turn out impossible to bear. In addition, for all this to happen, we must be walking rightly with the Lord, fear Him, listen to Him, and be sure that we are prompt to serve Him and not men. If we do not fear Him, keep His commandments, nor listen to His voice, and if our mission is not to serve Him, we will not be able to achieve any of these things, because He first prepares us, and once we have the right heart, He gives them to us.

Making all these desires true comes with many responsibilities. The words sleeping, singing, and travelling can be easily pronounced, but when we take on the challenge with a mature heart and the right character, they are hard to experience.

Focusing my attention on what God's servants achieve through their trips and experiences was not allowing me to see the sacrifice there is behind it all. Anyone can travel, but it is God who qualifies us to trust us with His plans and makes sure that this does not harm our hearts.

If you are a dreamer and you feel that God called you to serve in full-time ministry and promised you the Nations, but you do not see anything happen even though you are working on it, you should ask yourself the following, "Am I approved by God?"

How can I be qualified by Him?

When faced with these questions, I personally answer this to myself: "The only way to be qualified is by committing to His purposes". God has plans and dreams for everyone, but not all of us may be able to achieve them, for these blessings are only available for those who commit to serve Him unconditionally - those who dare to walk in His ways and have God in their hearts above any other thing, those who bravely guard His commandments and obey them without expecting anything in return.

God thought of many things for us, but He allows us to develop and experience them according to our maturity. One of the examples I sometimes use in my conferences or sermons has to do with universities, schools, institutes, bar associations and government offices: when they need a person to represent the institution, they always evaluate who is best prepared for such a task.

When it comes to representing a university, they will trust a teacher more than a student. They may send an outstanding student who has sacrificed, studied, and committed, but they never choose someone who is not trained with the knowledge needed to efficiently represent such an institution.

Many employees, students or teachers may be jealous or feel envious of the one who was chosen for the task, but he received this outstanding position as a gratification for the effort and sacrifice he made to train himself, and not everyone is willing to pay that price.

Those who have prepared in a remarkable way, who possess the necessary attitudes and skills and who also show quality in their work will be chosen to represent their institution.

No company will make the mistake of sending someone who can put the company's prestige into question but will take care of efficiently preparing someone capable of doing it in the best way. And that's how God works, too.

He has plans for each of us, but we must bear fruit before His presence, not before men. Fear of the Lord is the most important thing alongside with being careful of having a vain or selfish heart. We should seek to be prepared for God's will to be fulfilled in us. Our priority should be to become a vessel of honor where God can deposit whatever He wants, and we can be efficient ambassadors of the Message of Salvation.

«PUBLIC ATTENTION IS THE BEST STAGE TO DIE TO OUR OWN DESIRES FOR RECOGNITION AND REVEAL THAT WE'RE NOT THE MESSAGE, WE'RE JUST THE MESSENGERS.»

In His Word, God gives us this wonderful piece of advice: "Work hard so you can present yourself to God and receive his approval. Be a good worker, one who is not ashamed and who correctly explains the word of truth" (2 Timothy 2:15 NLT).

Our Father looks for many ways to prepare us but sometimes we are not willing to embrace that commitment - we are simply motivated by the benefits we can get from carrying God's word.

The life of a minister is not as easy as many believe. A minister must have constant communion, because that is the only way to become one with the Father and be approved for His mission. If we are children of God and carry His Word, we must listen to His voice; otherwise, we will act out of our own will and that is where our downfall begins, as well as many other mistakes.

The committed servant must learn to listen to God's voice to be able to carry the raw, pure, and true Message to this generation. The man who loves the Lord must be committed to live a life of holiness, close to God, because we are the tool that He'll use to carry His Word to the people. And if something is not well with us, not only will it be obvious, but we will also force our emotions to make something happen, ignoring and despising the essence and the genuine move of the Holy Spirit.

The Scriptures say: "By their fruit you will recognize them" (Matthew 7:16 NIV). I repeat: God qualifies us. If we want the benefits and everything that seems to be fun, we need to have a firm commitment. He is the One who sends us. A consecrated life is what precedes going to the Nations. A life of intimacy with the Lord prepares us to administer His grace, and when the Lord places His grace upon us, it will flow over those around us, without struggles. That grace will represent us, qualify us, and send us out.

Many people have a desire to go to the Nations, but they are not necessarily prepared to represent the Kingdom of God, and He is not willing to send someone who will make Him look like a fool.

Nations also have representatives who stand up for the values, principles, laws, and foundations of the country they represent: these are called "ambassadors". You may not be able to represent the country you were born in, but you are called to represent Christ to the Nations, so you must make sure you are trained in the knowledge of the person of Jesus, what He represents and can do.

"We are therefore Christ's ambassadors, as though God were making his appeal through us. We implore you on Christ's behalf: Be reconciled to God" (2 Corinthians 5:20 NIV).

Do not be one of those who sends himself out and – unfortunately - end up ashamed, for he does not find open doors, just closed ones. Some will ask me: If I am investing my money, my time, and my talent in serving God, why is nothing happening? To which I respond with much humility and love: God will not open the doors to you if you only have the desire to obtain the benefits without the commitment that He demands.

«GOD HASN'T CALLED US TO BE CELEBRITIES. HE CALLED US TO BE HIS SERVANTS!»

NOT EVERYTHING IS THAT SIMPLE

Sleeping, singing, and traveling - that is what I thought it would be like. It was not until I started traveling for the first time that I learned that, although everything was as exciting as the experience of taking a plane, eating, singing, getting to know different countries and cultures, I felt that the more I served God, the greater the responsibilities I received, so with every new opportunity I needed a higher level of commitment.

As the days went by, the itineraries began to look fuller and busier. But what seemed so pretty at first - like the planes or meeting new people and cities - was no longer so. It was beautiful to see the reward of so many souls converted to Christ on each night of worship, but the lifestyle behind all of it was not comfortable. What people see on social media is the nice part. Sometimes they assume that everything is perfect when in fact all these experiences also carry difficulties.

Just for you to imagine what I am talking about, I will describe a travel itinerary to you, one of the longest I have ever had.

Depart from the Dominican Republic at 4 A.M. and arrive at Atlanta at 10 A.M. Leave Atlanta to get to another city at noon. Hotel checkin at 3 P.M., then go to sound check, radio stations, and return to the hotel to get a shower and leave again for the concert. Finish the concert, take another plane to get to another city and do the same thing all over again. Land in that new city at 6 A.M. after having slept three or four hours on the plane. Give some interviews, subsequently do the sound check, and sing that same night. We have been through this time and time again. Since I have been part of the Barak ministry, I have visited approximately two hundred cities around the world. I have done over a hundred trips per year.

To share the Word of God is beautiful, only when we do it with purpose. Otherwise, everything is very depressing, for the heart dries up, joy leaves and nostalgia and tiredness arrive, along with the desire to see your family and be a normal person who just stays at home and is free from commitments.

If we are not truly prepared to know what we will do from the beginning, or the reason why we are sent, our greatest desire could turn into our greatest frustration from one moment to the next when it becomes true.

There is nothing sadder than the moment you must get on a plane, and you are tired, sometimes without even eating, but even if you are exhausted, you must give your best to join a crowd that is thirsty for God and dance and sing with them.

This leads me to analyze the reason why there are so many suicides in the secular artistic scene. Great artists such as Whitney Houston, Avicii, Robin Williams, Kurt Cobain, and many more, who were at the peak of their careers with very demanding itineraries, made the decision of committing suicide. Being an artist is more about giving than receiving. The only possible way to put up with this lifestyle is knowing that, if God does not send you, it is impossible to keep up with the rhythm. This is the reason why secular singers take refuge in drugs, applauses, people and even money. But when all this fades away, a void remains that only God can fill.

The admiration and affection of the people around you is amazing, but I confess that on some occasions I have not been at my best, because even if I still have not had time to comb my hair, or I have just woken up, they approach me asking for a picture. Every place I go, people I do not even know seek to engage in a conversation to know more about my life. I do not think we should not make new friends, but when this happens several times a day, it becomes demanding and exhausting, since you must always show kindness because of the calling you are representing.

All these details fill your heart with worry and if there is really no vision, if you are only doing it to show yourself off, or you are just looking for the applause, your heart will not be filled, you will still be tired, you will not find rest for your anxiety nor fill the void that only God and your family can fill.

I think that is one of the reasons why there are so many artists who do not know Christ. They make bad decisions because all these burdens get to their hearts, leading them to experience moments where they do not want to meet or greet anyone, or they do not want to sing, until they feel the desire to put an end to their lives.

There are days when I feel the exhaustion of flying for so many hours, and moments where maybe I was not able to eat or sleep well. However, I must go on because I have a commitment to fulfill. If it were not for the strength that God gives me, I would have a helpless life. But I have no choice! God chose this for me, I even dreamed with it, and when difficulties arise, I must always value the beauty of this blessing and do not let it become a source of frustration.

I have learned that sleeping, singing, and traveling is the nice part, what most can see externally; but behind all that, there is a maturity that must come with the commitment related to obeying the voice of God. There's where God becomes stronger in our weakness. In the moments, when you are sad and alone in your room - if you are close to Him and qualified by God - He will remind you what your mission is.

When you have a goal, God multiplies your strength, not to try to please people or receive applauses, but to minister salvation and healing. The Holy Spirit gives you life every day. When we are qualified and prepared, He Himself will endorse the mission He has given you.

DIARY OF A FREQUENT FLYER

Itineraries are extensive and there are many things hidden, like never ending flights, entire days without eating, lost luggage, delayed flights, etc. Sometimes, the sound equipment that we specifically need does not make it on time for the concert. In some countries we have not been able to board the flight due to the great crime there is in those areas. We have been in Nations where we have been mistreated against for the color of our skin - among other things.

One of the worst situations that I have been through is that I woke up learned one morning after a very busy day to take a flight. We were headed to a country - whose name I will keep to myself - and when I got there, all the guys from the band were admitted into the country but because of a small detail in my passport I was sent back home. You can imagine! Everyone was expecting to see Barak; the stage and sound equipment were ready, but the lead singer had had to return home. That was very difficult and embarrassing.

We experienced another difficult situation on another occasion. We left the Dominican Republic and took a connection flight. We had to do Customs in the United States, which took us more than three hours. Of course, we missed the flight to our following destination and the only flight available arrived exactly sixty minutes after the time we had set for the concert. Being the only alternative, we took that flight and arrived our destination at 12:30 at night. What a special day!

We left at approximately six o'clock in the morning and arrived eighteen hours later. We showed up at the concert in the same clothes we were traveling with, without a chance to even take a shower. That is how we had to minister. Now, it is just a beautiful anecdote, because even though it was really late, the crowd did not go home and waited for us so that we could worship together.

But that is not it! I saved the most unpleasant part of this calling for last, which occurs when I must travel anywhere in the world and leave my wife and kids for several days. Being away from my babies is one of the most painful things when I travel.

Due to the number of commitments, I have missed many of their birthdays, graduations, first days of school, wedding anniversaries... Oh wow! Would you believe me if I told you, I did not arrive on time for the birth of one of my children because it overlapped with tour commitments? And what if I told you that we are still solving their registration documents, since one of my kids does not have my last name because I could not arrive on time for his registration at birth? However, I'm not worried that one day my little ones will look back and remember that Dad couldn't be with them in the important moments, because whenever I can, I bring them together to tell them about the commitment that we as a family have to carry the Word of God, and that even if Dad isn't always at home, we're all part of the purpose and the reason why "I do what I do".

Every day I thank God because my children have understood this (even though they miss me a lot) and have followed my steps and those of my wife to prepare for ministry, love the Father above all things, and preach the Gospel.

Anyway, I cannot deny that I sometimes cry when I am away.

and one of my babies tell me he misses me, or calls me to ask, "Daddy, when are you coming home?"

On certain occasion I felt heartbroken when I returned from a long tour and my kids welcomed me with great joy after several days of missing me, only to receive the news that I had to leave again the following day. When I told them that I had to leave again early in the morning, they were very sad and could not understand why I had to leave if I had just arrived. This is painful!

My beloved wife, Ana, does not always take it very well but at the end of the day she comforts and encourages me. She reminds me every day that our family is fulfilling a purpose, that perhaps it is me whom the Lord has sent to do a job that has an impact in the Kingdom, but in the end, she knows that, even if I am the one who must travel far away, the sacrifice that we do as a family is what changes the lives of many people. God could not have given me a better wife and suitable helper, so understanding, supportive and someone who loves God above every other thing. This makes me fall more and more in love with her, because I can leave home confidently, knowing that a mature, responsible, and God-serving person is in charge and will keep our home safe if I am far away.

Of course, my wife and I are in constant communication. She often tells me how important I am in the house and how the children change and behave when I am away. Every day we improve as a family and as a home, despite not having the lifestyle of an ordinary family. Being instruments of God is a beautiful privilege and a great gift. Each sacrifice we make is worth it because our kids see the example and are inspired to serve God with everything they have. We might sacrifice a lot of the time that we could be together, but when we share as a family, we thank God for the privilege of being His instruments to make Him known to the world.

One thing I must explain to you is that not everyone may be ready for this. My marriage has had to mature a lot - my wife and I have prayed incessantly that our home will be founded on the rock and that no circumstances can bring it down. If you have a calling from God, you must understand that He will not put that ministry over your family. On the contrary, everything will work for the growth of that union.

In my case, we took care of building the foundations of our home in Christ, and the first place right after God is for my family. Ana and I have understood that it has been a specific call of sacrifice with the understanding that God is the One who sustains our home.

«NO MATTER THE CHALLENGES WE FACE, IT'S A PRIVILEGE TO BE AN AMBASSADOR OF THE KING AND BEING ABLE TO KEEP THAT LEGACY IN YOUR HOUSE.»

THE COST OF SERVING

If serving God does not cost us anything, then we are doing something wrong. As sons and daughters of God, we must value what He has placed in each of us. Being a minister must cost us something, because if we do not guard the greatest treasure that we have, we could lose it.

You should ensure that your dreams and desires are not based on benefits, luxuries, or impressions to prove "what God does with you", but rather that they are based in "what God does in you". Looks can be deceitful and not everything that you see is pleasant or satisfying - like "sleeping, singing and traveling" - but deserves a greater commitment with the Lord than what can be seen externally.

All the disciples were called to spread the Message, but they did not fantasize about being recognized, being famous artists, or stars of the Message of Salvation. On the contrary, their hearts were completely focused on the commitment they had to share the Message that transformed their lives. Jesus said to them, "Go into all the world and preach the gospel to all creation" (Mark 16:15), and they took it seriously since, thanks to those twelve men, a great part of the world has heard about the name of Jesus.

I am struck by what Paul said in Acts 20:24, "However, I consider my life worth nothing to me; my only aim is to finish the race and complete the task the Lord Jesus has given me—the task of testifying to the good news of God's grace" (NIV).

I am amazed by his level of commitment, that he even detracted his own life just so he could do what he had been called to do. Many times, we believe that our value is given by a ministry, or that we are defined by the position of recognition for what we do. However, it is the complete opposite. Having a commitment with God is solely and exclusively about Him; we just carry out the service that was entrusted to us by announcing the message of His grace.

When we are called, we must understand that the commitment we make to God is not giving up until the end, even if things do not turn out the way we thought they would. The fact that the call is burning within you does not guarantee you that you will never feel exhausted or drained at some point, but this call is for the brave ones, who do not give up because of their needs or conveniences, on the contrary, they do things understanding that it is not about them - it is all about Jesus.

Your money, talent and influence might place you in a position where you feel you have reached your dream. But it will not be until you see the not-so-pleasant side of all this that your commitment to the Lord of never giving up will be tested.

If you are qualified and able to do everything for Him until the end, get ready to sleep, sing and travel!

Let's reflect together

My dear friend, I can assure you that serving God and answering to His call is the most beautiful experience you will ever live - and at the same time, you will have to go through tough situations. As I have already shared, the life of a worshiper, pastor, or evangelist is not as easy as some believe. It really takes spiritual, emotional, and physical strength to respond to the calling. Service has no schedules or distances and knows no night or day - we should simply serve with love and joy because that is our call.

1– Do you feel God has called you to serve Him as a worshiper, pastor, evangelist, teacher, or prophet?

2– Are you willing to face the difficult moments that come with service, or just enjoy the beautiful part of the calling?

Let us reflect on each of the chapters that I have shared with you, and you will realize that, to reach my purpose, I had to go through many sleepless nights, lonely rooms, and disappointments from certain people around me. You should know that service is composed of everything that is beautiful and everything that is difficult. Because it is a great thing to long for.

There's a sound in you

Chapter 10

Chapter 10

THERE'S A SOUND IN YOU

I'M SO GRATEFUL TO GOD AND TO YOU, my dear friend and reader, for having given your time to create a space where God, you, and I have forged a bond through this reading. I bless your journey and the perseverance you have had to get to this point.

If you are reading the words of this chapter, it means you have walked with me through a journey where I opened my heart and made my experiences known to you in long conversations - from the crisis that I have been through, to what the Lord has done with me. I also told you about my passion for music and how it became my way to serve God, that, despite the highs and lows, nothing has been able to stop my unwavering commitment to the fulfillment of the Great Commission given to us.

On each page I described the unusual ways and harsh circumstances in which I learned to sing and to develop my abilities to serve God with the utmost excellence. I may have described many experiences, moments and key places that marked the life of Robert Green, but now I will tell you something very particular that happened in my early days, so that we can then talk a little bit about you.

I am pretty sure that by walking in my shoes through this book you were able to discover tools inside of you that you did not know about - like how valuable gifts and talents are - but now I want to talk to you about something that I consider to be the most important factor to achieve our goal of serving God the right way.

In this last chapter I want us to discover the authentic, original, and unique things that the Creator has placed inside you. If you still have not done it, I would like to begin by letting you know that there is no one else like you in the whole universe. You are special and God made you unique!

Unfortunately, as servants of the Lord, we have made many mistakes by neglecting our authenticity and misusing our talents, whether out of ignorance or unawareness of what God wants to do in us.

One of the main things that you ignore but that has surely stalled you is called "comparison", and from now on you must consider it your greatest enemy. At some point we have all used it to evaluate how good or bad we are, according to the parameter that someone else establishes. And in the ways of the Lord, that must not exist in us.

Comparisons make us highlight what we lack, what we do not have but others do. In many ways, this could bring anxiety and even depression for it keeps us from understanding what God has deposited in us.

Trying hard to look like someone else is to work in vain, since we were individually designed with different talents and gifts, and along with the failure to do so comes the frustration of failed attempts seeking to be someone we are not. We reproach to God the fact that we cannot grow in what we do; this is because we are paying attention to other people's ways instead of risking it to discover what God has placed in us.

Let me tell you how I discovered and valued what God had placed in me, so that you can see yourself reflected in my story and together we can discover the sound that is in you.

When I became deeply passionate about singing and began to show my talent publicly, I realized that there were numerous prototypes of singers that I began to compare myself with and, somehow, I lost my authenticity, and I even questioned the voice with which I sang.

So many times I repeated phrases in my head like, "You have to sing the song that way, just like this singer does" or "You aren't singing it the way he does, you must do it like him and sound like him", or "The style that is being used must be different from what you sing", completely losing my originality as an artist and as a minister of the Lord.

By trying to be a good copycat of someone I admired, I lost the ability to see that the Creator had placed something authentic and unique within me, and I needed to find it.

Somehow, the fact that I did not look like Marcos Witt, the singers of Hillsong Ministry, Marcos Vidal, or other great servants of God whom I compared myself with, brought me insecurity. But the pressure increased when those around me encouraged me to imitate them with the recommendation that by doing so I would find success, since our artistic surroundings positively valued those who shared the same style of certain international and famous singers, while I - in my particular and different way of doing things - did not fit in.

I experienced so many disappointments and frustrations that I embraced the idea that I was never going to achieve anything with my voice. Until one night, alone with the Lord in my room, I burst into a sea of tears and expressed the frustration that was oppressing my heart. I sat on the floor and with the greatest dissatisfaction and quite an attitude of complaint, I said many things to God.

I even complained about the way I sang. Can you imagine that? I was whining in the face of the Master of the universe and wisest of all, about the decision He had made of gifting me that voice. It was evident that I had completely lost my identity. I said to the Lord in discontent, "My voice is too hoarse, it doesn't sound like anybody else's, and no one likes it".

WE'RE ORIGINALS, NOT COPIES

God made you to be exclusive, and this pleases his heart. When we deviate from this, we can truly offend God's decisions and go in the complete opposite direction to where He wants to take us.

The devil is a professional imitator and deceiver. So much that he wanted to "be like God". Which is impossible! And to this day, his intention is to imitate everything that God has created in such an original way, as well as to divert everything that He has deposited in us to push us away from the purpose for which we were created.

His forgeries have sneaked in every area of human life: music, art, culture, economy, sexual identity, family, and church, among others. Satan, the deceiver, and father of lies, wants to distract you, and lock you inside a fake life, making you believe that you were born to be just like someone else. Do not allow him to do this! You are unique!

My complaints were complete nonsense! How did I want to be a copy? How could I think at the time that what was deposited in me came from leftovers? I was tricked into thinking that God, with the incredible talents He had to give away, had created better singers and that He had left only scraps for me. Wow! The enemy had influenced me a lot!

Despite the haughty way in which I talked to God to protest about nonsense, He was merciful with me. Surprisingly, from one second to the next, the Holy Spirit took that same mouth with which I was complaining so much, made it shut up and used it to speak to me. Amid my brokenness, I began to speak words from behalf of the Holy Spirit in a supernatural way; words that answered every single one of my questions. God is so beautiful! With much patience and love He took time to reveal to me the importance of what He had deposited in me.

In an unexplainable way, with grace and truth, the voice of the Spirit dismantled my complaints with questions, "How can you think that I have put something in you that I have not designed, valued and conditioned to be perfect for your life? How could I have saved the worst things for you?"

Such simple questions left me speechless. I did not know how to answer to the One who knows it all. I remained silent. But then He said, "There's no one like you in the whole universe, you have an original purpose and calling. Do not compare yourself to anyone else, nor allow them to compare you to others. I took the time to design every single detail in you, and I didn't put them in you because I had extra ones, but because that sound that is within you pleases my heart, perfumes my throne and gives me joy."

This experience helped me understand that every resource God placed in me was valuable, and even if I did not like them or thought the world, leaders, my friends or even my family did not like them either, they had been placed in me to impact the Nations.

After being confronted with such a revelation, I was able to understand a powerful truth that changed my life and has the potential to change yours too: God deposited an original, unique, authentic, and perfect sound within each of us! "For we are God's handiwork" (Ephesians 2:10).

No matter how well or bad you sing or play an instrument, if you understand that God has placed in you the special grace to do it, do so and perfect what you have, without losing your essence.

Many insecurities might constantly suggest who you are supposed to look like and that can make you always feel unhappy with yourself; you might dislike your own face, your hair, your physical appearance, but God looked at what you have, analyzed it, and created it knowing what would look better and more beautiful in you to reflect Him.

Give thanks for everything that the Father has put in you, whether big or small: Your soprano or contralto voice, mezzo-soprano, or baritone, whether you play the piano or the trumpet, or have any other talent for God related to arts. Develop what you have because it is what the Father thought for you when He designed you and it is the sound that will fulfill its purpose. Let it flow in you!

YOUR OWN SOUND

If you ask me, "Robert, what should I do to find my own sound?" First, acknowledge that everything God created is good. "For everything God created is good, and nothing is to be rejected if it is received with thanksgiving"(1 Timothy 4:4 NIV).

Put your eyes on Jesus and run straight into the Potter's arms whenever you feel frustrated or confused. Allow Him to shape, like clay, each one of the systems of your body, talents, thoughts, and your whole being. "Yet you, Lord, are our Father. We are the clay; you are the potter; we are all the work of your hand" (Isaiah 64:8 NIV).

When an electronic device stops working, it is the manufacturer who knows exactly how to reset it, above anyone else. That happens with us too. When our life gets messy, only God can reset it, making all things new and all things work for what they were created.

You must know the tools available to you and ignore the loud voice of your insecurities and lack of identity. Do not hide inside your shell. Give God the chance to expose what He has placed inside of you. It is better to pay little to no attention to human flattery, for it does not define if what we are doing is right or wrong. Tune your heart to God's heart, explore and discover the unique qualities that He has placed in you. And remember you are special. Take advantage of the platforms you have available to serve and let your sound out.

I remember my pastor, Santiago Ponciano, looked at me and said, "Fly. God is going to do something great at any time. Get ready, believe in what He has deposited in your life".

I am so thankful for my pastor, that even despite all my doubts, he gave me a chance in church to grow and work on my insecurities! With his support, by allowing me to lead worship and encourage what God had put in me, I began to discover my own sound. He trusted me more than I trusted myself and, seeing my potential, he appointed me to lead worship in the different weekly services. This certainly helped me to discover and unlock what God had placed inside of me.

I thank God for what my pastor did at the time, and I believe it is a great example that we all should imitate as part of the Church. Just because someone is related to the pastor or to somebody in the leadership team does it mean they must get the opportunity to lead worship, preach or serve in any area of church. We must support every talented young person, who may still be in doubt of his or her potential, but who carry a sound that God wants to use to bless and minister to His people.

If we motivate and encourage what God has put in them, we will help many believers already trained by God to bring out their best. Activate your own sound and with what you carry, join those of us who, in different ways, carry the same message.

United in prayer, we must intercede for the youth to awaken to its own sound - that special and original sound that is so characteristic of them. Let us pray that we keep the same essence by showing Jesus, but with the different talents that we have. "Each of you should use whatever gift you have received to serve others, as faithful stewards of God's grace in its various forms" (1 Peter 4:10 NIV).

The last part of this verse reinforces the fact that God made us all different, for God's grace in its various forms" are the different ways in which God is manifested in our lives. There are not two like you, and there are not two like me either. God's grace has millions of different forms, and He made the time to place something specific in everyone to show His glory. "If all the parts were the same, it could not be a body. But now there are many parts, but one body" (1 Corinthians 12:19-20 NLV).

When I was a kid, my parents taught me about Jesus in many wonderful ways, and that is why I bore fruit. With their help, I was able to open my spiritual ears to listen to the personal plan God had for me, to fully manifest everything that I was able to do with the specific gifts He had deposited in my life. Now that I am a father, I have learned about the delicate balance we need to have to guide them in the path of salvation.

Our kids need to be guided by the will of God and not at our own whims. We must guide them to the Lord, not so that they may be just like us, but so that He guides them in His purpose.

We are responsible to motivate our children without getting in the way of God's purpose for their lives. If our kids are grounded in God, we must move aside and let them make their own decisions. We can only give them advice, so that they go to the Lord before they make any decisions, without any pressure from society, their family or even a ministry.

If you have children, encourage them to discover the special talents that God has placed in them, and to boldly fight for that purpose, if they are sure that those are the dreams that the Lord has for them.

LET'S TALK ABOUT YOU

Now, I will ask you some very personal questions. Do you know the sound there is in you? Do you recognize the unique capacity that He has deposited within you so that you may please Him? Do you serve with the unique and special gift with which you were designed to bless others?

Not all the answers to these questions should be "Yes". Perhaps there are still many things you have not discovered about yourself, but I guarantee that God will use every experience, decision and process you go through to bring out the best of you and strengthen your character so that you can show with authority - and without any insecurity - whatever He needs to expose from your life.

Most probably you have been mocked, pointed out, or even shamed by so many people that do not perceive the greatness of what God has deposited in you. However, God, in His vast ability to create, has made the perfect decision to place a sound within you that goes beyond your voice, your musical instrument, your preaching skills, or whatever art you may feel identified with.

Our God does not waste time, He owns it; and from now on, while you are still in the process of discovering the sound that is in you, I have no doubts that the best days of your life are ahead of you, where you will see His glory manifested through what you do. You were designed with gifts and skills to impact Nations and generations.

I often say that "There's more to hear than what we've already heard and there's more to see than what we've already seen". God is an endless God - there is always something new to discover in Him! You know what I mean by this? If you still have not seen what He will do with you, it is because He's preparing you for something bigger and better than what He has already done.

From today on, seek for the accessible and generous heart of God. Be genuine and He will give you even more than what you can ask for. Become an apprentice and loyal follower, one who pursues the perfect example of the Father. Become His right hand, someone He can trust, in whom He can deposit His biggest plans and dreams to be glorified in the world.

I have told you a story that continues, but to this day God has allowed me to understand who I am in Him, what my calling is, and recognize that there is nothing I could do to make Him love me more. It is by His grace that I have been chosen, and I have obeyed out of my love for Him.

Make count the sacrifice of love that He paid for us; walk with Him every day of your life and let out the sound that is in you.

There will be many ups and downs in the journey of your life, and it is completely normal for all human beings to walk through them, but never forget this: God has a purpose with you

Let's reflect together

Discovering your own sound is something you must achieve alone with the Lord. The words and experiences that I have recounted throughout these pages might have helped you, and I really hope they did. But I pray that you may find your own sound - no matter your age and whether you are a man or a woman. I am not just talking about musical notes - which I love and have intoned for so many years - but I am referring to the sound of your calling, whatever this might be. You carry a unique DNA; you have unique fingerprints and are an original creation with a distinctive sound. Your job and personal challenge are to discover it. Look for it without ceasing and be the best that God has called you to be. Whatever the ministry you were called in His purpose is, be unique and original. By being yourself, you affirm and confirm that God has a purpose with you.

LETTER TO THE HEART

WHO ARE YOU?

Who are you when you get off the stage? Who are you when the spotlight turns off? Who are you when the performance comes to an end?

Who are you when the show is over? Who are you when you finish your speech? Who are you when the camera is not pointing at you? Who are you when no one is taking a picture of you? Who are you when no one is praising you? Who are you when the applause does not come? Who are you when your ego is not comforted? Who are you when your smile fades? Who are you when the mask of "happiest person in the world" falls off? Who are you when you are alone? Who are you when God says "No"? Who are you when you no longer look that good? Who are you without social media? Who are you when you are not surrounded by people who like, share and comment on all your posts? Who are you when you are not the one imparting and ministering? Who are you when someone disciplines you? Who are you without a microphone or instrument in your hands? Who are you when you are far away from what is advertised and magnified?

Because to God, what is essential is still invisible to the eye but reflected in the heart. Someone who is a secret but is loyal and faithful is much more valuable for the King than someone who is explicit but indifferent to the values and foundations of the Kingdom. It is not about how many billboards carry your image, but how many of your attitudes people can see and read and encounter Jesus through them. The most beautiful way to live is not exhibiting out "truths", it is by letting others discover who we really are through the footprints of our actions and behavior. The Lord does not care about your fame, status, exposition, or glamour. He is interested in your life, not in the camouflage you use to survive. He is interested in being inside your room when you close the door with repentant in your heart, willing to change your character; He is interested in that man or woman who wants to be led by Him and is thirsty to see a transformation. My friend, God cares so much more about your inside than He cares about your outside.

www.ingramcontent.com/pod-product-compliance
Lightning Source LLC
Chambersburg PA
CBHW072117050526
44107CB00098BA/283